About the Author

NURDAN GÜRBİLEK, one of the foremost cultural critics in Turkey, is the author of *Living in a Shop Window* (1992), an analysis of the cultural dynamics of the 1980s in Turkey. Her other publications include *Shifting Shadow* (1995) and *Homework* (1999), a collection of essays on modern Turkish writers. She is also the author of *Bad Boy Turk* (2001), an analysis of some of the significant images and tropes in modern Turkish literature and popular culture, and of *Orient Lost* (2004), which explores the sexual anxieties accompanying the Ottoman-Turkish literary modernization. Her last book, *The Language of the Wronged* (2008), is a collection of essays on Dostoevsky's 'underground tragedy' and its counterparts in modern Turkish literature.

The New Cultural Climate in Turkey

Living in a Shop Window

NURDAN GÜRBİLEK

Translated by Victoria Holbrook

ZED BOOKS
London & New York

The New Cultural Climate in Turkey: Living in a Shop Window
was first published in 2011 by Zed Books Ltd, 7 Cynthia Street, London
N1 9JF, UK and Room 400, 175 Fifth Avenue, New York, NY 10010, USA

www.zedbooks.co.uk

Selected essays from *Vitrinde Yaşamak* and *Kötü Çocuk Türk*
© Metis Yayınları, 1991, 2001
Copyright © Nurdan Gürbilek 2011
English-language translation © Victoria Holbrook, 2011

The right of Nurdan Gürbilek to be identified as the author
of this work has been asserted by her in accordance with
the Copyright, Designs and Patents Act, 1988

Designed and typeset in Monotype Fournier
by illuminati, Grosmont
Index by John Barker
Cover designed by Rogue Four Design
Printed and bound in the UK by CPI Antony Rowe,
Chippenham and Eastbourne

Distributed in the USA exclusively by Palgrave Macmillan, a division of
St Martin's Press, LLC, 175 Fifth Avenue, New York, NY 10010, USA

A catalogue record for this book is available from the British Library
Library of Congress Cataloging in Publication Data available

ISBN 978 1 84813 486 7 hb
ISBN 978 1 84813 487 4 pb
ISBN 978 1 84813 488 1 eb

Contents

INTRODUCTION

Cultural Climate, Personal History

I

THE ESSAYS IN THIS BOOK aim to analyse the various aspects of the cultural climate that came to dominate Turkey in the wake of the 1980 military coup. I say 'various' because if one is to understand that climate, one really must take up, all at the same time, several contradictory phenomena, even entire interlocking cultural climes. Even now as I offer this book to readers scarce familiar with them, my head is crowded with scenes that belie that unavoidable, and Pollyanna-ish, trope of Turkey as a bridge: a bridge between East and West, Muslim and Christian domains, modern and not-so-modern societies – a jumble of scenes even I find hard to connect. Pictures of Turkey that don't jibe.

True: Turkey is a land of military coups, repressive policies, violations of human rights – but also a land whose cultural pluralism ill suits that picture. Land of the world's biggest shopping malls, tallest hotels, gaudiest shop windows, but also of inaccessible villages, deserted farmlands, and cities ringed by shanty towns. Land of international biennials, international festivals, international exhibitions, but home to people sunk furiously in nationality. A country where books are banned, seized from bookshelves and destroyed, but where people believe education is the key to every problem and all but fetishize reading. Land of people who for years feared to use the word 'Kurd', only realizing there was a 'Kurdish issue' when children sent off for military service did not return home, but also of people whose favourite pop singers are Kurds. Land of people proud that their republic recognized the legal rights of women at its founding, but who feel constantly threatened by femininity. A country where homosexuals are treated brutally, but homosexual singers are made into icons. Land of strong religious communities where people expect the army to protect them against religion's threat; of people who boast of a great empire's legacy yet lost their ties to that cultural inheritance long ago; of Europhobes who have long felt European and are sick to death of begging at Europe's gate. Land of people who cry they are victims of the West while victimizing their own 'minorities'.

Turkey really does seem to be a land of contradictions, not only to those who view it from outside but to those who live here as well. It is devout and secular, modern and not, repressive and liberal, rich and poor, central and peripheral all at the same time. Perhaps most importantly of all, Turkey is both victim and oppressor. Yet it would not be right to extract a 'land of contradictions' from these contrary images, candidate to replace the 'bridge' cliché that seeped into tourist brochures by way of diplomatic lingo. For several reasons. First, contradictions lie at the foundation of almost all cultures, not only those which like Turkey lie beyond the capitalist centre; if we do not see them it is because we do not look attentively enough at the contradictions slumbering there, above all those constituted by liberalism and authoritarianism, civilization and barbarism, urbanity and modern *naïveté*. Second, in Turkey all the polarities I have mentioned are closely related in particular to strategies of power which crystallized in the 1980s; so they must be historicized, not offered as natural contradictions of an unchanging Turkish climate. Third, even when they arise from Turkey's provincial position in the world, we must not think of the polarities here in isolation from the dynamics shaping the rest of the world, but on the contrary in concert with them. For if we do not, we will immediately be nailed down by another cliché, a fantasy of the East as at best exotic, at worst uncanny; an image of Turkey as a backward, dark, savage land yawning from the other end of the bridge, where a completely different set of laws obtain. In fact Turkey constructed these contradictions not by itself, but in ongoing relationships, partly of conflict and largely of compromise, with others, above all its great other, the West. In any case, I will in these essays be speaking less of a local climate entirely Turkey's own than examining how a new climate, one intimately related to changes taking place in the wider world, has drawn Turkey under its influence. I will take an approach which allows us to see Turkey's otherness but also to understand what kind of relationship with the rest of the world that otherness emerged from. And for that reason I would like these essays to be read not merely as the tale of a far-off land of darkness but of Turkey's West within.

II

On 12 September 1980 Turkey awoke with a military coup to the most repressive period of its recent history. The army took over the government in order to silence the voices of opposition and suppress in particular the opposition left, which had in the 1970s achieved a mass status never seen before in Turkish history, thus establishing 'economic stability' on the stage of a society cleansed of all tensions, all protest, and all opposition legal or illegal. In order to 'place upon sound foundations a democracy unable to control itself', political parties, political associations and trade unions were shut down; the constitution was altered. In order to rescue Turkey from 'deviant ideologies' and 'destructive and separatist foci', dossiers were created on nearly 2 million people; hundreds of thousands were arrested and hastily tried. Over five hundred people were sentenced to death, fifty of them executed; over a hundred died under torture; thousands lost their citizenship. Books, magazines and films were destroyed by the thousand. Within two years the military institutionalized their position of control over political power and then withdrew. The leader of the junta, Kenan Evren, served as president of the Republic from 1982 to 1989. In 1983 elections the Motherland Party came to power in a discreet collaboration with the military. To this day the leaders of the junta have not been tried.

The climate of profound fear established by the 1980 coup had as much of a constitutive effect on cultural life as the legal arrangements it put in place. Turkey entered a period of severe repression, whose effects endured after the military had gone. Yet the climate which left its imprint on Turkey during the 1980s cannot be understood merely in terms of repression, prohibition

4

and a politics of elimination. What distinguishes this from other repressive periods in Turkey's recent past, what made it a fracturing point of not only economic and political but also cultural life, is that during those years Turkey became the site of a great transformation which the concept of repression alone cannot explain. Another way to put it is to say that repression came to the fore along with another strategy, apparently its precise opposite, one promising freedom in the cultural sphere. This is the starting point for some of the questions I will try to answer in the essays here. How is it that this most repressive period in Turkey's recent history could have offered itself as an age of opportunity in cultural life? How could a period governed by prohibitions have called itself into being with the promise of freedom in the cultural sphere? How could this promise have been so effective, so believable? What had Turkey repressed of its former self while bringing its modern culture into being? How did these repressed contents return? And, more importantly, what did they return as?

I said that 'repression' alone is not sufficient to account for the new climate. For in the 1980s the media gained the tremendous power they still have today in Turkey, the advertising industry developed with breakneck speed, big capital took up a determining role in culture, and the market became the constitutive basis of culture. These were the years when Turkey was rapidly transformed into a consumer society, a society of images, a society of desire; the years when huge shopping centres were built one after the other in the big cities, when gigantic advertising billboards and glittering shop windows succeeded in creating the image of a society of plenty, and Turkey promptly took the place deemed fit for it within globalizing capitalism. That is why, as I analyse the cultural climate of Turkey in these essays, I will speak of two different cultural strategies. In order to periodize the Turkish 1980s, one must be able to distinguish these two fundamental, at first glance contradictory, characteristics. On the one hand, the period was framed by repression; state violence made itself nakedly felt, a great many people were put in prison; social opposition was suppressed by force, the 1970s radical left was wiped out and prohibition left its stamp on cultural life. But on the other hand, the 1980s were years when another strategy of power went into effect, if not for the first time, then for the first time in such a way that it pressed its imprint into the culture as a whole; one less familiar to Turkey, a more liberal, more comprehensive, more inclusive strategy of power, aiming to encircle by speech rather than silence, to transform rather than prohibit, internalize rather than destroy, tame rather than suppress. It was a period of denial, censorship and silencing; but also one of promise, provoking desire as never before. One strategy operated on the basis of repression and exclusion, or forced abnegation; but a second sought to arouse, internalize and tame. Turkey was silenced, the right to speech cut off; but 'A Speaking Turkey'[1] offered new channels and frameworks for speech. From the point of view of institutional, political and humanitarian ends, it was one of the most severe periods in Turkey's recent history, but at the same time a softer, freer era of cultural pluralism when people were relieved of their political responsibilities and began for the first time to speak in the cultural marketplace for their own selves, rather than in the name of some political mission. On the one hand, a politics of silence prohibited use of the word 'Kurd'; on the other,

Turkey's most famous arabesk pop singer in the 1980s was 'The Emperor' İbrahim Tatlıses, a Kurdish construction worker who rose to stardom to enjoy all the opportunities wealth in the big city could offer. Turkey's famed transsexual singer Bülent Ersoy was banned for eight years, prohibited from singing in public; but popular news magazines stubbornly plastered their covers with homosexuals and transsexuals and invited them to confess all to the public. Freedoms were more restricted than ever before, but people had perhaps never felt so free; they tasted a freedom from institutions and the pleasure of surrender to this world, in short the freedom to consume to their heart's delight.

Certainly repression was severe during the first years of military rule; its latter half was relatively relaxed. But it would narrow our horizon to define the two strategies chronologically, to say the one came first and the other followed later. For throughout the 1980s, neither strategy ever took the other's place; it was rather that they came into being each calling upon the other, each dependent upon the other for its effectiveness, each owing its legitimacy to the other. The first knew it would not be able to rule society by prohibition alone, that it would not take its place in the capitalist world that way; but the second knew, when it stood with the free market against the state, that it really owed its existence to a market freed by state violence through military coup. It may be that Turkey's fate for a good while longer will have to be sought in the double quiddity of this interlocking weave. In the land of liberal politics sprung on the heels of military coup, the two cultural strategies join in silent solidarity, partners in crime even when they disavow one another. What the first represses, the second provokes, transforms and includes. What the second provokes, the first represses.

Two strategies, two forms of power; within a space of time short in the history of any society, a liberal politics promising freedom of speech settled snugly into prohibitive policies of state. What made the 1980s the scene of a great transformation whose effects still endure in Turkey's cultural life today was the fact that those years combined two parallel universes, and, more importantly, brought them into being in compromise. The State of Emergency Region Governorship's[2] violence and patronizing posture towards the Kurds, the ban on Bülent Ersoy's performances and the media's fever to make homosexuals heard, the prohibitions in the cultural sphere and funnelling of capital investment into culture, the destruction of institutions giving voice to the demands of the masses and the emergence of a powerful mass culture: all are varied faces of the same period.

That is why if the cultural climate of that period be described first of all as 'repression of speech', it must then be characterized as an 'explosion of speech'. And there really was, from the late 1980s on, an explosion so widespread as to create the illusion that repression was a thing of the past. Prohibitions continued, yet people began to speak with an appetite the like of which had never been seen before. The 'explosion' in fact come about through the intersection of several factors. Culture became subject to the market on an unprecedented scale, the infinite image was swiftly thrust into circulation by advertising, and a new *vox populi* came into being as popular news magazines became a feature of the publishing sector. What all these developments had in common was that, while they arose outside the boundaries of official culture, and partly in reaction to it, they owed their existence to a market freed by the coup. None of this explains, however, why I describe the phenomenon as an 'explosion'. I choose the word because here we must discuss not only the provocative strategies of the market and how they incited people to speak, but also repressed desires, energies which had been inexpressible before, silenced contents which rapidly, suddenly, emerged on a new cultural ground. That is precisely what happened in Turkey in the 1980s. Groups unable to express themselves within the founding Republican ideology began to speak, groups that had no place in the Kemalist modernizing design: Kurds, 'minorities', Islamists – in sum, the provincial population. But it was not only them; women too found a new voice. Women's speech had been restricted according to their part in the Republic's modernizing design, and to a great extent within the 1970s' narrative of the left as well. Homosexuals, almost never heard of in public, began to speak for themselves in the same years. Each of these different sectors began to speak, doubtless in different forms, to greater or lesser extent, and according to the varying opportunities afforded them, but suddenly without the framework of a grand political narrative, without recourse to the opportunities such narratives afford but also free of subjection to a narrative, perhaps not for the first time, but for the first time in a powerful way. That is why the period was such an important fracturing point in Turkey's recent history – the 1980s were the scene of this cultural explosion. If I keep returning to those years in the essays in this book, it is because I think we really must assess the significance of this fracturing point well if we are to understand polarities in Turkey today. If Turkey appears to those who view it from outside to be both a land of religious communities and a society of spectacle today, if the provincial Turkey we always thought of

9

as poverty-stricken is able to acquire investment capital today, if religion and capital, faith and finance, religious conservatism and liberalism, 'the private sphere' and the realm of spectacle – all of which we have only just begun to think of at the same time – are comfortably joined today, we should seek the causes in the great transformation of the 1980s.

III

I have spoken of varied aspects of the 1980s cultural climate, and of how so many things came about simultaneously in what may be considered a short space of time. That variety led us down many blind alleys. In the years right after the coup, when Istanbul suddenly acquired the character of a city of festivals, a friend of mine pitched the question: 'Could it be said that the 1980s' festivals were good for drowning out the screams rising from the prisons?' The question seemed to me too harsh, too point-blank, as it did to everyone else present. It hadn't been intended to provoke soul-searching but it did, and no one wanted to answer it; whatever we said would be wrong. My friend answered his own question: 'It would be wrong to say that', he said, and then added quickly, 'but also wrong not to.'

Sometimes you have to make do with half-truths. Maybe the contradictions were not always so sharp, but they have always been there. And in several realms at once: political repression and glittering shop windows, terrifying civil war in the east and provincial Turkey on the rise, the practice of torture and the call to individualism, the silence of prohibition and the hunger for speech, cultural standardization and multiculturalism, all shared one stage framed by these two different strategies, which I think still count on one another for survival in Turkey today. In fact the 1980s are important not only because they make it possible for us to see how different strategies work together through compromise, but because they point out the limitations of the liberal strategy. The local came more to the fore than it had at any time in Turkey's recent history; but the explosion of the local obviously took shape under global pressures. Those were years when people acquired a sense of place; but this inevitably brought on an ideology of the local and a power struggle over whose local it really was. Cultural identities could now express themselves without cover of a grand narrative umbrella; but the political common ground upon which those identities could transform one another had already lost its power to support them. The 1980s were years when culture ceased to be something arising spontaneously, and demanded autonomy more than ever before; in a sense, daily life culturized itself. But, on the other hand, the realm known as culture was overly exposed to the pressures of the world market and lost its autonomy, perhaps for the first time in such a decisive way. The masses in Turkey were more visible than ever before, thanks to the explosion of 'low culture' in this period; but at a time when the institutions which allowed them to give voice to their demands were wiped out, desires, hopes and longings were penetrated by the culture industry more thoroughly than ever before. It was perhaps the first time that intellectuals spoke for themselves to such a great extent, but also the first time they had so categorically lost their authority. The 1980s were years when inner lives, sexual preferences and private pleasures came to the fore and people were inclined to bare their souls. But, on the other hand, private lives were cannibalized; norm and deviation, mainstream and margin were probed and named, and despite all their variety subjected to the crudest of social codes. There was a drive towards individualism, the more ferocious for its belatedness; personal wishes deferred could now be expressed more easily; but at the same time what we call desire became more subject to the desires of others than ever before, and often what remained was merely a desire to consume. People discovered the body and its appetites, and were able to speak openly of sexuality; but the realm known as sexuality was encircled and penetrated as never before. The particular, the personal and the private found ample opportunity for expression; but the domain of experience which arose on these foundations was in danger of losing its particularity, perhaps more definitively than ever before. The 1980s were years when feminism advanced in Turkey, when women made more efforts to develop a language of their own and complained that woman was a being without a name; but the domain known as womanhood was more besieged by a politics of speech than ever before, named as a new domain and in a sense discovered. The notion that the private is political was first voiced then; but it was often overshadowed by the publicity of private life as politics fell from esteem. There was more interest in the past than ever before; but the past became a pop history cleansed of its historical-political burden. Language was freed from its political responsibilities and allowed to define itself as a game, but at the same time it became completely random, arbitrary; language became its own ground. All of this concerns literature intimately. Literature was searching for its own autonomous principles in the 1980s, far from the pressures of politics; but it too, like private life, experience, femininity and the provincial, was left exposed to pressures that threatened its autonomy, above all the familiar pressures of the market.

In sum, we had to live through a great many things all at the same time in Turkey. The extraordinary conditions of the period of repression, the rapid transformation of Turkey into a consumer society, Kemalism's loss of its monopoly on modernity, Turkey's discovery of its 'minorities' and own Eastern, provincial, Muslim face. No small number of changes, positive and negative, intersected within a short space of time to create a great transformation displayed on varied fronts of culture; changes in how people perceived themselves and how they were named, how they dressed and what they read, in the structure of sentences and the meaning of words, viewing habits and the language of the news. It was in order to understand this great transformation, looking to affect Turkey for long years to come, that I wrote some of the essays in this book.

IV

Shop windows do not glitter long in this world; it is even harder for them to keep their sheen in a country like Turkey where there are few means to satisfy desires aroused to such extremes. And so in the short space of ten years, as the world slid from 'multiculturalism' to 'the clash of civilizations', a progressive hardening occurred. The promise of freedom and the society of desire, which had seemed so convincing at first, began to show their seams. These were years when shop windows lost their glitter, the lightness of being faded away, and the exuberance of the 1980s gave way to a darker sense of the uncanny. In the 1990s unfulfilled promises aroused rancour, not desire, and once again the city street was etched into consciousness as a site of crime while the struggle over the city's resources was carried out in a much more tense environment, under much harsher conditions.

It is no coincidence that a second explosion which would gradually captivate Turkey from the 1990s on was an explosion of 'Turkishness'. It is truly difficult to think of any other period in Turkey's recent history when Turkishness was so emphasized – with its sense of injury, introversion, wounded pride, anxiety, rage and resentment. The causes were certainly contemporary, and, to that extent, reactionary. Turkey's old middle classes were forced to share the resources of the metropolis with provincials who day by day became more visible in the marketplace, day by day acquired a greater share of capital, and who moreover derived their power from religion, now an ideology more difficult to call into question. There was a line of defence developed here against politicizing Islam, but also against the now clearly audible voices of large parts of the population never before taken into account, above all the Kurds. Children joyfully sent off to the East to war against separatist Kurdish guerrillas returned as corpses. The European Union was an adventure also embarked upon enthusiastically, and it too ended in frustration; turned back from Europe's gate, Turkey closed in on itself with wounded pride and took refuge once again in its own Turkishness in haughty self-sufficiency – 'I'm enough for myself.' Efforts to redefine Turkish identity put their stamp upon the 1990s and 2000s.

It is this second explosion that forms the background for the essays on Turkishness here. But rather than limit the discussion to contemporary issues, I will try to take a closer look at the *alla turca* impasse which has plagued Turkey's modern culture. Let me make clear right away that when I speak of 'Turkishness' I do not mean an autonomous or originary condition which can be defined in itself, some backwardness resisting every assault of the modern, or an essential reality alleged to identify this country's true natives. On the contrary, I speak of a double bind which was from the start shaped in relation to the modern world, a link of double engagement which has always produced antithetical emotions in the cultural sphere, of an abandon and summons to return to the self, an enthralment and fear of losing the self, admiration of the foreign and xenophobia forced to live side by side in a single soul, a sense of inadequacy and grandiosity, victimhood and defiance, and finally a political–cultural milieu that persists in inciting those feelings. A fate which leads some in Turkey to think of themselves as 'dandies' and others as 'provincials', continually reproducing the native–foreign antinomy as a defence not only against the world outside but against the world within.

It is the novel which best describes that fate; moreover, when we discuss the limitless anxieties of authors we can view our own anxieties from a certain distance, with a more critical eye. For that reason, in order to make that fate better understood, I will look closely in these essays at certain figures who form an important component of popular culture in Turkey, yet are not at all strangers to literature – suffering heroes, wounded but noble children, bad boys locked into resentment, and effeminate snobs. I do so with a fundamental question everyone in the uncanny world of today should ask of their own national identity, and which, being from Turkey, I will put this way: where do 'Turkishness' and 'evil' connect?

V

Finally, I would like to say a few things about the form of these writings. Some of the essays in this book set out from an item in the newspaper, some from a photograph, some from a pop song, and some from literary works. But these writings are not free of emotion; however much they are products of intellectual effort, for me they are also parts of a process of mourning. For while writing them I was trying to understand why the opposition left of the 1970s had not been revived, and also to digest that reality. But these years were traumatic not only for those coming from the left opposition but for many others as well, and I was also trying to make of them more than something approached with emotion alone, more than an object of rage, regret, or merely a feeling of relief, and analyse them as a historical period when possibility and impossibility lived side by side.

I realize that to try to do all of these things at the same time, especially in the essay genre, which is so fragile and, I think, susceptible to grandiosity, overly burdens the writing. But while writing these pieces I saw no other way on the horizon but the essay; for I had to give place at one and the same time to cultural climate and my own personal history, to theoretical analysis and the work of mourning, to analytic attentiveness and the feeling of recoil I was experiencing as I wrote – in short, to concepts and to a life experience which does not always fit easily into them. Furthermore, I was struggling with a history whose contents sorely tried the truths I had made my own; those truths had to be re-examined in the light of traumatic experience, not merely new information. One must ask again: What gives the essay its power?

While Georg Lukács collected his essays in *Soul and Form* at the beginning of the last century, he was asking himself if one is entitled to publish such works, if they can give rise to the new unity of a book. In 'On the Nature and Form of the Essay', the introductory piece, he likened the essayist to a precursor awaiting the coming of someone else:

> And if that other does not come – is not the essayist then without justification? And if the other does come, is he not made superfluous thereby? Has he not become entirely problematic by thus trying to justify himself? He is the pure type of the precursor, and it seems highly questionable whether, left entirely to himself – i.e., independent from the fate of that other of whom he is the herald – he could lay claim to any value or validity.[3]

That other. For a generation that discovered intellectuality not on its own but through others, and believed it could be sustained only through others, this was important, I think. And for that reason I too wish these essays to be read as writings biding their time while waiting for an other. Let this not be misunderstood: it is not because an other who will invalidate these writings has appeared on the horizon to smile from afar; on the contrary, it is because I think it necessary to preserve the important thought of an other when that other has not appeared. After a political experience in the 1970s when everyone wanted to be something all together, Turkey promised all of us many things. In the 1980s it promised we could take pleasure in things we had done without until then, promised us the weightlessness of action performed not in the name of any mission, and that we did not have to be of the high culture to enjoy the world of opportunity; and much more in that vein. But unfortunately as all that had been repressed before returned, it expressed itself through whatever channels it found. It would be difficult to say that these channels were always innocent ones. I am thinking of the shock a young friend of mine felt when she realized in the early 1980s, at a time when dissidents in Turkey felt themselves squeezed between the repression of the state and the less visible but more comprehensive pressures of capital, that a dreadful piece published in one of the big newspapers had been written by a friend of hers. She was a leftist, she was used to the evils of the state; more to the point, she was accustomed to an idiom suitable for analysing only the evils emanating from there. She just could not understand how someone whose opinions she'd shared could be mixed up in something bad, how a dissident could be co-opted by the market. Nor have I ever been able to forget what an older and certainly more pessimistic friend said around that time: 'Just wait a little longer, the day will come when you will see the faces of your friends behind all the evils around you.'

So that is how personal history has seeped into these writings. And why it cannot be said that these essays surrender to their topics impartially; I suppose their critique, like their defence, is embedded here.

It is said that humanity sets itself only those tasks it can handle. There may be two ways to interpret this. One is to say that we can find a way to overcome our problems no matter what they may be. The second must register limitations. Yes, humanity sets itself only those tasks it can handle, if this world we live in is itself an answer; in that case we must think again: well then, what was the question?

I have already exceeded the limits of an introduction. One last point. The chapters here are revised and expanded versions of essays chosen from my books *Living in a Shop Window* (1992) and *Bad Boy Turk* (2001). Early versions of most of them were first published in the journal *Defter*, of which I was a founding editor. *Defter* readers know that its editors had little to promise others and at best tried to resist in hope. What made these writings possible was that hope, which I shared with the others who brought out the journal for fifteen years. If in the end I came out of it with a book, it is because I could not do more.

ONE

Living in a Shop Window

I

IN A 1929 ESSAY Walter Benjamin wrote of a hotel he stayed at in Moscow. He noticed that almost all the doors to the rooms there were always ajar. At first he thought it was a coincidence, but gradually he became ill at ease. Finally he learned that the rooms were occupied by Tibetan monks who had taken a vow never to be in a room with the door closed. This 'moral exhibitionism' impressed Benjamin. He decided that 'to live in a glass house is a revolutionary virtue par excellence.'[1]

Benjamin visited Moscow in 1926 and after a stay of two months returned disillusioned to Europe. He wrote those words at a time when the revolutionary atmosphere in Russia was gradually shutting down and issues were beginning to be addressed behind closed doors; he must have seen 'moral exhibitionism' as a guarantor of freedom. How much has changed since then. The doors closed then were opened in the Soviet Union by state policy in 1985. And in 1989 the Berlin Wall was torn down. But in the new order of the world in which we live, the question is still left hanging there. Will we be able to find a guarantor of freedom in the politics of openness today? Can we hope to have from moral or political exhibitionism what Benjamin hoped for? Can we see it as a revolutionary virtue to live in a shop window?

II

A thick fog spread over Turkey after the 1980 coup; doors closed, walls rose up, many things became invisible. But when the fog had dispersed a little, we realized that each and every thing had been transformed into a sharply focused image; the relationship between seer and seen had become one of spectatorship, and speech itself had become a shop window. Right from out of the fog there emerged a society in which many things existed because they were shown and to the extent they were seen; they acquired value because they were displayed and to the extent they were viewed. It changed the relationship we constructed with the city, especially Istanbul; Istanbul was transformed right before our eyes, step by step, into a site of spectacle. The mayor of Istanbul, Bedrettin Dalan, played the leading role in this process; as soon as he took office in 1984, in a ritual open to the public, Dalan all but tore down Istanbul and built it anew.

Previous local administrations had torn down Istanbul and rebuilt it anew; they too had made this a ritual open to the public, a spectacle which firmed up their image in the public mind. But the Dalan difference lay not in how he was able to transform his redirection of the unearned income in the city, his reshaping of the city according to the demands of the groups who controlled that income into mere show, but in how he was able to appear to be resolving the complex problems of a metropole by virtue of this show and make this image convincing. Dalan spoke, for example, of making the colour of the Golden Horn – then stinking, polluted slime – as blue as his own blue eyes. It is no accident that, during years when all things in Turkey acquired value to the extent they were transformed into shop windows, even the eye itself became a metaphor not for the seer but for the seen; not for the viewer but the thing viewed. For in those years not only foreigners but Istanbul's own residents began to look upon their city as a site of spectacle, reducing the neighbourhoods where they lived, the ground on which they walked, to a point of view accidentally theirs, and realized their lives had value only to the extent they were viewed. The people of Istanbul were now expected to look upon their own city from outside, with the eyes of a foreigner, and wait for others to discover their value in this great city which more and more resembled a shop window with every passing day. True, the European foreigner had long been important to modern Turkish society, but rather as a model to be emulated. The difference now was that the foreigner became a tourist, a customer, someone to curry favour with rather than imitate.

I am thinking of what Corbusier said about the street in 1924. Walking along the Champs-Élysées one day, he realized how much the traffic was bothering him; loud cars speeding by prevented him from enjoying his walk. He recalled the Paris of twenty years before and the boulevard as he strolled it during his student years: 'The road belonged to us then; we sang in it, we argued in it, while the horse-bus flowed softly by.' The same Corbusier saw that he could view the city from a less familiar vantage, from the point of view of traffic, from within an automobile. He identified himself with the forces bearing down on him. 'The new man', he wrote, needed 'a new type of street', 'a machine for traffic', 'a factory for producing traffic'. When he looked at it that way, the street must have lost all meaning for him. He said it plainly in 1929: 'We must kill the street!'[2]

As Istanbul was gradually transformed into a world city in the 1980s, its residents experienced a similar transformation. The first of the giant shopping centres built in those years was Galleria Ataköy. I found it odd at first when a Galleria shopkeeper likened the huge shopping centre to the Kaaba in an interview with a journalist. But the comparison gives a clear sense of how people related to the Galleria. It is far from the city centre, and one has to travel to get there. One does not go there as one goes to Beşiktaş Market, or to shops in the underpasses of Karaköy and Aksaray, where one stops while passing by; or the arcades of Şişli and Beyoğlu stores one visits on the way home from work or after seeing a movie or play. The Galleria is a place one can visit only as one visits a shrine. But in fact it is neither market nor shrine. No traditional, no familiar concept can quite account for it. In many ways it is like a picnic site that fills up with families, children and all, on weekends; but most of all it resembles a fair where goods are displayed; where one makes the pilgrimage to Commodity. It not only transforms the act of shopping from a natural part of city life into an end in itself, making of wares an exchange value whose use-value is all but erased; it changes significantly our relationship to the thing viewed. It gives people the opportunity to be tourists in their own city – by completely wiping out the potential for constructing relations of familiarity with a place.

III

The foundations of our contemporary viewing habits were laid in the previous century. Georg Simmel wrote that with the growth of mass transit, people found themselves in the situation of having to stare at one another for minutes or even hours on end without exchanging a word. It must have been cause for great anxiety at first, to look at people and things one did not know, to look and not recognize. Simmel maintained that a person able to see but not hear is much more troubled than one able to hear but not see. There is something here special to the sociology of big cities: the superiority of eye to ear is the distinguishing characteristic of relations between people there. The resulting anxiety brought people to place an unprecedented distance between themselves and the people and things they viewed, and remain indifferent to them as they never had before. Simmel emphasized that the distancing had become most noticeable in large city crowds: 'This is because the bodily proximity and narrowness of space makes the mental distance only the more visible.'[3]

There is also the other side of this whole process. We also know that people in big cities view unfamiliar things as a kind of game relieving boredom or distress. Benjamin wrote that when Baudelaire visited Brussels, he complained there were no shop windows in the city:

> Among the many things that Baudelaire found to criticize about hated Brussels, one thing filled him with particular rage: 'No shop-windows. Strolling, something that nations with imagination love, is not possible in Brussels. There is nothing to see, and the streets are unusable.'[4]

Here there is an opportunity afforded only in the distance a life lived in the big city can offer: momentary glances, the meeting of eyes and chance encounters are possible only when the surface of the city becomes more important than its historical depth. Only there can the *flâneur* stroll. Yusuf Atılgan began his 1959 novel *The Idler*, the first *flâneur* novel in Turkish, with this sentence: 'It suddenly occurred to me that she too might be in the crowd spilling over the sidewalks. The knot of tension inside me melted away.'

Baudelaire spoke of boulevards where rich and poor come eye to eye. He described glittering boulevards lit by gas lamps, lined with cafés whose gilded cornices and broad mirrors dazzled the eye. And of the poor who gazed upon all this wealth, 'their eyes wide open as carriage gates'. In the years Baudelaire wrote *Paris Spleen* (1869), Paris was undergoing the greatest transformation in its history. Neighbourhoods and people were displaced, rich and poor districts set apart; the city was divided. Opened up by means of broad avenues, the contrast between classes in the city became visible. Baudelaire described the poor as 'a family of eyes' in his 'The Eyes of the Poor'. The poet's gaze before shop windows is that of an idler dispelling his gloom. 'The idler does nothing', he wrote in his notes, 'but ridicule.' Yet we also know that he joined in the 1848 Revolution. He was on the barricades even in the radical days of June. Years later he looked back on what he called his 'intoxication in 1848' with detachment, though not indifference. The Revolution, he observed, 'had only been amusing because everybody built utopias just like castles in Spain'. But there was something drawing him to the barricades: as he put it, 'A taste for revenge.'[5]

IV

Those who find themselves in the Istanbul underpasses of Kara-köy or Aksaray notice that crowds tend to gather in front of shops selling cassette players. But most people, particularly if they have recently arrived from rural areas, don't really look at shop windows intending to buy; they gaze at something there which is alien to them, which they wouldn't be able to afford to buy anyway – 'technology' on display. They do so to the sound of the loud music that echoes down all underpasses. In the 1980s it was 'arabesk', which emerged as the pop music of this city-become-shop-window.[6] Adept at miming and maiming musical styles out of context, arabesk owed its power as much to the existence of a mass of people cut off from their traditional culture but not yet part of urban culture, alien to both, as to its ability to weave a surface by sampling genres so historically diverse (Arabic music, taverna music, Turkish music, pop, folk and march) as to be impossible to synthesize.

Simmel defined the stranger 'not as the wanderer who comes today and goes tomorrow, but rather as the person who comes today and stays tomorrow'.[7] If the tourist is someone here today and gone tomorrow, the stranger is someone here today who cannot leave tomorrow, someone who cannot go back. This is the stranger in the city to whom arabesk calls. It is the music of those who cannot return to the village, who are no longer villagers but not yet city dwellers. But it is also the music of revolutionaries who spent long years in prison during the 1980s and could not return, when they got out, to the world they had left; the music of men and women still imprisoned though set free. Yet, unlike the gaze of the tourist, theirs comprehended both 'inside' and 'outside', for they were able to line up the segments of their experience, or rather the symbols representing the different time segments of their experience, side by side. Arabic music and Turkish music, the *saz* lute and the synthesizer, fatalism and revolutionism, religion and protest: the stranger's gaze took in all as a sequence of images.

Arabesk was first the music of the road, played on long trips, in inter-city bus terminals, roadside restaurants, and minibuses working routes between shanty towns and city centres – places neither 'inside' nor 'outside'.[8] For arabesk is anyway not the product of a tradition, a cultural totality, or even a synthesis in the true sense of the word, but rather a genre of music open to symbols of different historical times, places and cultures. In a way, it is able to internalize because it has no 'insides', because it can transform words and music into a surface woven of symbols. That is why it is the music of nobody. The arabesk listener hears something which is not hers, which is alien to her, but not anyone else's either; a music neither Turkish classical nor folk nor pop. Here is what makes arabesk so inviting, what makes it call out to the strangers of the city: in it styles and genres belonging to different times and places can be quoted freely. It can shift from one style to another without spending much time on any; revolutionary lyrics, marching tempo, the intricate rhythms of Turkish folk songs – all are just samplings. Perhaps fans of Orhan Gencebay, the 1970s' creator of arabesk, took his songs to heart when they listened to him then, but the arabesk of the 1980s had long since turned Gencebay himself into a quotation. The more widely known arabesk styles of later years gradually abandoned all claim to sensitivity, or authenticity, becoming themselves imitations of arabesk. Turkish lyrics could be sung like Arabic lyrics in these songs, for example; arabesk with English lyrics could even be sung with Turkish intonation.

Songs could be sung with what seemed to be a regional accent but was in fact the non-existent accent of a non-existent region. Language can only be transformed into a mere element of mimicry, into an effect, in a society where the relationships between place and history have taken on the character of spectacle. The language we call arabesk offered us sites where we could wander among others, without staying long. Just as these places could be tavernas or meyhanes, they could just as well be political demonstration marches or the 'evenings' 1970s' revolutionaries used to organize.

Arabesk is where the before and after cultures of 'the person who comes today and stays tomorrow' are reconciled: both one and the other. And also the place which divides her whence she came and where she now remains, the place where she breaks away from her former culture and resists the new: neither one nor the other.[9]

v

The newly developed advertising sector in Turkey played an important role in making our relationship to the world one of spectatorship. For promoting a product is less a matter of truly describing its characteristics than creating an image of it, making a reality of an appearance. In fact the dissociation between the makers of a product and those who sell it occurred much earlier. Products were displayed in shop windows before the development of advertising; in those days too wares were set before us in such a way as to conceal the fact that they were the products of labour. Advertising did not create a new world; a new break was merely experienced in an already ongoing process. There was a complete break between those who fashioned a product and those who promoted it, between the familiarity on which knowledge depends and the know-how of promotion. And the frontiers of the society of spectacle expanded considerably; newspapers, television and huge billboards transformed the entire city into a gigantic advertising screen.

Politics was one of the spheres of activity where this change in Turkey was most obvious. In election campaigns of the 1980s the identity, the image, the style a party offered to view became more important than its programme for the first time. Gradually the relationship between a party's programme and the image it projected became more arbitrary, more gratuitous. To be sure, this show mode was not limited to election campaigns. Turgut Özal, who set up the first government after the coup, announced that he would withdraw from politics if he did not gain the votes he wanted in the next election. The Istanbul mayor Bedrettin Dalan declared, when a weekly magazine published news of corruption in the construction of the Istanbul metro, that he would take the magazine to court. But Özal did not withdraw from politics; nor did Dalan take the magazine to court. Once these incidents were reported by the press, it was as if Özal had withdrawn by saying he would, and Dalan had filed a suit by threatening to file one. Helpless, one could protest these things by saying 'I will set myself on fire' – that too is a gesture – and it would be as if one had set oneself on fire. For a society which consists merely of gestures compels opposition to become mere gesture as well.

On 8 November 1988, precisely at the time when I was writing these lines, a woman whose son was condemned to death in fact doused herself with gasoline and tried to burn herself alive: the final helpless act of a person trying to save one she loves when all avenues of action are blocked. But unfortunately, in a world where words take the place of action, and action is received as words, no one pays any attention.

VI

Several of the subcultures developing in the West since World War II have grown into something more like symbolic parties of opposition. Punks, skinheads and other influential dissident groups preceding them put themselves forth as a show, a collage made up of contrarian images, defiant styles and symbols abhorrent to established order. These groups often emerged from working-class and migrant neighbourhoods, and decorated their bodies symbolically, trying to turn themselves into a display clashing with the established order. They violated the language of the master symbolically; they experimented with stealing symbols of the dominant culture and giving them antithetical meanings. Like the minibus driver in Turkey who turns his vehicle into a bizarre, contrarian space by decorating it with homey pieces of lace, gnomic proverbs, protest slogans, and signs reading 'In the name of God, the Merciful, the Compassionate', they tried to turn their bodies and the places they lived into shop windows disturbing the eye in a society of spectacle. Modern consumer society was constructed with a limitless empire of signs, and they tried to tear down that empire from within by means of what Umberto Eco has called 'semiotic warfare'.[10]

Symbols live a migrant life too. The *Caretta caretta* sea turtle, which today serves as the symbol of an environmental movement,

30

could be the logo of a huge tourist agency tomorrow. The theme of the 1970s' Turkish left-wing slogan, 'To lay claim to the past and march on the future', now appears in the advertising campaign for a bank. Che Guevara has long since been turned into a fashion icon. The punks who took on the European establishment have been added, with all their transgressive accessories, to advertising's limitless stockpile of raw material. The designer Mary Quant said that she was influenced by the modes of dress adopted by another subculture, the Mod girls of the 1960s. Just as subcultures steal the symbols of the dominant culture and work to create a symbolic counter-system, the consumer society cleanses those same symbols of class and historical content and returns them to the market. And the market allows opposition symbols to circulate freely as long as its own principles remain in force.

The Situationists influential in France in 1968 were the first revolutionary movement to point out that society had become a society of the spectacle, a society of signs. Their response to Eco's phrase, 'semiotic guerrilla warfare', was to be expected: 'Words forged by revolutionary critique are like partisans' weapons: abandoned on the battlefield, they fall into the hands of the counter-revolution and like prisoners of war are subjected to forced labour.'[11] They were right; but even that did not prevent the year 1968 from being transformed, twenty years later, into a symbol of rebellion cleansed of all historical content, a '68' minus its first two numerals.

VII

So, must we say that everything consists merely of naming, of images?

Shop windows always signal plenitude. But what makes this plenitude possible, what brings it into being, what is expended and exhausted to create it, that is not shown in the shop window. Shop windows conceal from those who gaze into them the fact that the wares displayed are products of labour. Just as the market equalizes forms of labour and reduces products to an exchange value, all the experience, lost opportunity and labour expended to make them becomes a mere image when society becomes a shop window.

There are nineteenth-century glass ewers displayed in the window of an antique store in the Istanbul neighbourhood of Rumeli Hisar. They were not sold in their day because they were considered defective. Their defect lies in the drops of blood consumptive workers blew into the glass. Now they are priced as antiques. Yet one should not forget: it may not always be others who put pain on display in a shop window. Those who suffer can themselves finally make a spectacle of their experience.

Marx spoke of the language of commodities, saying that every commodity was a 'social hieroglyph'. Is it possible to decode those hieroglyphics and observe that images in the market have different languages? Immediately various images from 1980s' Turkey come to mind. Turgut Özal constructed a new type of image in the public mind by means of his political gestures. Another type of image was offered up by factory workers who shaved their hair, worked barefoot and went on hunger strike, seeking symbolic means of resistance when they lost their right to organize in unions. Can one say that those images are the same? When one decodes the hieroglyphs of huge shopping malls or arabesk music, of election campaigns or hunger strikes, will they be found to have the same meanings?

I started out on this essay with a metaphor and spoke of how society in Turkey was transformed into a shop window. But it seems that in order to understand this phenomenon today, we must finally put aside metaphor and look directly at the shop window itself. Shop windows in Turkey have never been so rich and the buying power of the majority so poor. We know this: 'The spectacle is *capital* to such a degree of accumulation that it becomes an image.'[12]

Will knowing this be enough to turn our gaze to a life beyond the shop window?

TWO

To Be Named

IT WOULD NOT BE WRONG to characterize the 1980s in Turkey as a period when experience was rapidly put into words. Many experiences formerly considered 'private' were put on the public agenda if not for the first time, then for the first time so obviously. As I mentioned in the introductory essay there was a great discursive explosion around the concepts 'private life', 'sexuality', 'generation' and 'individual'. Lifestyles were categorized; comprehensive typologies were constructed – 'women living alone', 'childless couples', 'the generation of '68', 'marginals', 'bisexuals', 'the arabesk audience', 'turbaned women'.[1] Various experiences to be acquired in modern life were encompassed by specific namings, specific images. Sexual tendencies were categorized; heterosexuals, homosexuals, bisexuals and transsexuals became popular subjects for magazine articles. Generations were named; the Freedom-loving Generation of '68, the Left Generation of '78, and the '88 Yuppie Generation were all differentiated with clear-cut lines. The years when the media gained new power, when the advertising sector began to put its stamp on the market, when the city was transformed into a site of spectacle, a sweeping scan of the field, a desire to name, a virtual roll call of culture took its place beside all of these great changes. Inner lives were opened up to the public, sexual preferences named, private pleasures combed through. Turkey entered a period of eager discussion about what was mainstream and what marginal, what was normal and what deviation, what was moderate and what extreme, who was lower and who higher.

To give something a name, to call it by a familiar name, always involves an ordering process; it determines the nature of the relationship to be had with the thing named. But in a climate where the external referents of language thin out, or more often do not exist at all, naming cancels familiarity right from the start; more importantly, it removes the possibility of the thing being known. It puts into circulation a word which incites and propagates as much as it constitutes and cloisters. The word is now the expression of an extrinsic construct; it determines its own speakers; summons them into a politics of speech whose boundaries are set; determines which metaphors and images should be used to describe experience; and finally it calls that which is spoken of to join its order. Before people can be called upon to reveal their private lives, their private lives must be named as secret. Only when sexuality is named as a dark, secret region of life can people be called to bring it out into the light of words. The regime of speech has now established its own familiar world; all speech will now take its place within that constructed familiarity. Because this discursive explosion and discursive politics we have been subject to since the 1980s has named looks, postures and pleasures within a specific order, turning experience into an object of prosecution, I will characterize it here by Foucault's phrase: 'incitement to discourse'.[2]

II

In *The History of Sexuality* Foucault took up the history of sexuality in the West since the seventeenth century not as a tale of repression but rather one of how the veil was drawn back from sexuality, how it was brought into discourse, willingly or by force, and made the object of a scientific–institutional discipline. Sexuality plays a determining role in modern society when, and to the extent that, it is spoken of. The literature of scandal and the school principal who demands that indecent fantasies be recounted down to the smallest detail – both are components of a mechanism making sexual confession a general rule for the whole of society. It is not (as was formerly supposed) that sexuality was denied; on the contrary, it was encircled and imprisoned by speech. Sexuality was brought out of the shadows and had speech forced upon it by means of interpellation techniques. Foucault's approach brings with it a way of understanding that in modern society power operates less by denial, restraint, prohibition or exclusion than by techniques of establishing, ordering, inciting and propagating; rather than repressing or annihilating, it distinguishes, makes visible and classifies.

Here I will read the story Foucault tells more as one of power structures which emerged in a particular historical phase of modern Western society than as a universal story of power. It is the story of the historical transformation which separated the liberal from the classical age in Western Europe; the process by which central institutions gave way to partial disciplines, by which discipline spread beyond the state to the entirety of society, and power acquired a more fragmented, more polycentric, more interpellative character; the story of how the power strategies of – to use a phrase Foucault probably would not much like – 'civil society' came about. The related question I will ask regarding Turkey is: How does Foucault's story provide us with a way to understand a very different history, that of newly forming power strategies in Turkey?

It is only recently that Foucault's story of modernity has acquired an analytical value for Turkish society. It is not enough that theory be brought to bear upon reality; reality must in some way bear upon theory as well. And that was what made the 1980s the site of a radical transformation for Turkey: a discursive politics on a more partial level, beyond the prohibitive discourse of the state, interpellative rather than prohibitive, provocative rather than repressive, made itself felt in the 1980s, certainly not for the first time but for the first time in a powerful way. Such questions as whether or not the operation performed in Turkey was 'disciplinary' or 'reforming' in the sense understood by Foucault, or how former structures of power resisted the new power strategies, are doubtless subjects for a separate discussion. But it is possible to say that as a result of the transformation experienced in the 1980s, 'the regime of discourse' Foucault speaks of came to obtain in Turkey, if by means of different mechanisms.

The first example I will give has to do with homosexuality. When homosexuality was taken up on a Turkish television programme called *Chronic Depression* in the mid-1980s, the

programme moderator seemed at first to be the voice of repression
to which we were accustomed, with all its judgemental moralism.
One often sees this type of moralistic approach today as well, in
the press, in the writings of columnists, and on television news
programmes. But there was an important difference in the *Chronic
Depression* moderator's approach, which heralded the advent of
a new type of figure in Turkish public life. He gave a name to a
kind of sexual experience which was certainly known but had not
been much discussed in public; he invited homosexuals to speak
on the programme and made them the target of an insistent,
even vulgar interrogation, and asked specialists to comment on
homosexuality as an illness. In one respect he was doing what was
expected of traditional power, but he was also inviting discussion
of homosexuality as something to be submitted to institutions of
rehabilitation. A kind of incitement to discourse had replaced the
prohibition we had come to expect from traditional power.

In *The History of Sexuality* Foucault dwelt upon two cases
demonstrating how people were made to speak of sexuality in the
West. In one, a half-crazy agricultural worker is caught fondling a
young girl in a French village in 1867. It was an ordinary incident
of a kind which often occurred in villages, but it set in motion a
series of power mechanisms all at once: the girl's parents turned
the worker over to the village headman, who turned him over to
the gendarmerie, who brought him before a judge, who turned
him over to a doctor, who submitted him to the examination of
specialists. The worker's skull and facial structure were examined,
and he was compelled to tell the whole 'truth'; first he was the
subject of a forensic report, and then put in prison where he was to
serve as material for a scientific discourse prying into every dark

corner of sexuality, starting with the perversions, analysing and recording judgements of what was normal and what perverse.

The same years were witness to testimony representing a new phase in the regime of discourse in France. The confessions of the anonymous author of the eleven-volume *My Secret Life* were not a response, voluntary or involuntary, to interrogation by any authority. On the contrary, the author's daily record of his sex life in all its detail seems the harbinger of a tolerance which would emerge only fifty years later. But however repugnant the author's confessions may have appeared to the authorities, the fact that he was able to put his experiences into words made it seem that all could be narrated within one and the same parenthesis of normality. It was as if the surveillance function of institutions, once deemed necessary to make normalization possible, had now pervaded speech itself. For that reason to put things into words was now to consent to surveillance – not by someone whose speech and its provenance are important, but by anyone and everyone capable of being the grammatical subject of speech without author.

There are certain parallels here with the regime of discourse which began to make itself felt in Turkey during the 1980s. But it must be emphasized from the start that varied forms of power one would expect to see develop over a period of three to four hundred years, and in some cases be left behind, exist side by side in Turkey all at the same time. This is true of the example concerning homosexuality I gave above. By exposing perversions on a state television channel, offering them up for public censure, the programme moderator used the prohibitive discourse we had come to expect of traditional forms of power;

but at the same time he incited those he insulted – in an almost charitable tone – to speech; he called upon them to confess their misery. Here were two different forms of power, accompanied by two different regimes of speech, operative at one and the same time. On the other hand, civilian specialists dissociated from the state's repressive apparatus also began to make themselves felt in Turkey in the 1980s, specialists who defined their political and professional identity in contrast to the state, as did a discourse taking up sexuality as an object of medical analysis and classification as well. It was in the same period that people began to be interpellated, by weekly news magazine articles such as 'Premature Ejaculation' and 'Sexual Frigidity', for treatment in newly founded sexual therapy centres. But here one must mention the existence of a third project, a third discourse, which wished to see itself as different from the forms of power coinciding with those two institutional practices: a more modern project, legitimized under the sign of 'individual freedom', which cleansed itself of all institutional baggage and involved confessions around subjects never before discussed in public, unless as themes of literature. The difference in this modern project – which included free description of sexual fantasy in frank answers given to journalists canvassing door to door with questionnaires on sexuality prepared by weekly magazines (with questions such as 'What are your sexual fantasies?' or 'What would you do if your lover were bisexual?' asked by journalists who suddenly appeared at your door) – was that speech was articulated to a discursive regime aestheticizing experience rather than a scientific discourse of classification. What is important here is less the experiences and feelings themselves than how they are enunciated within a discourse of confession. Speech illuminating regions once left in the dark, and thereby thought to be freeing, now carried out the surveillance function itself, independent of any authority wishing to know. This development corresponds to the most advanced phase of the European history Foucault recorded, the sovereignty of incited, decentralized speech. But what is striking in the Turkish case is that people in a society to which the religious culture of confession is alien would have been so ready to speak frankly, so lacking in resistance to that modern strategy's interpellation.

These three different regimes of speech reigned together in 1980s' Turkey at almost the exact same time. But the interesting thing is that while these forms of power were creating their own historical realms in the West, they engaged in a harsh struggle not only with what they came to rule but with past forms of power as well. To win this battle meant to become hegemonic and, in a sense, un-namable while naming others – to become an invisible form of power. It was precisely this hegemonic character that Roland Barthes indicated when he defined the bourgeoisie as 'the social class which does not want to be named': 'the bourgeoisie has obliterated its name in passing from reality to representation, from economic man to mental man.'[3] Only by virtue of this invisibility, this 'ex-nomination', could the bourgeoisie speak for the entire society, name in its name, cleanse objects and relationships of their historical content and constitute its own natural, universal lexicon, thereby empowering itself as a silent norm. The new discursive regime that began to make itself felt in Turkey in the 1980s seemed odd, even caricature-like, partly because this invisibility of power was not fully achieved;

more often the various forms of power operating simultaneously could not assert themselves as a 'silent norm'.

But there is another important difference. In the West, the history of the lifting of the veil from private life was accompanied by the transformation of that zone into an object of systematic, analytical, institutionalized knowledge. The medicalization of sexuality was one of its most striking expressions; sexuality was made the subject of a discipline. But in Turkey, however much the specialists who tried to medicalize sexuality, defining what was normal and what not, were able to make their voices heard in newspapers and weekly magazines, most of them who saw society as a body to be rehabilitated did not hesitate to offer their disciplines in service to the state. Speakers at a 1985 Istanbul symposium on the rehabilitation of 'terrorists' in prisons, for example, included not only psychiatrists, specialists in pharmacology and neurophysiology, attorneys of criminal law and the director of the state department of forensic science, but the ministers of justice and domestic affairs, and international terrorism experts as well. In Turkey efforts to rehabilitate society still proceed hand in hand with the central power. For that reason it would not be wrong to say that the fundamental dynamic of the 'incitement to speech' experienced in 1980s' Turkey was the verbalization of private life within a discourse of liberation, in response to a call to individualism, independent of any authority seeking to know or rehabilitate. What put its stamp on the process was less an institutional authority which insisted upon knowing than the readiness of voluntary narrators to describe frankly their sexual fantasies, seeing in their confessions a potential for liberation, and respond hungrily to the questionnaires of a press culture seeking to create new arenas for journalism. As a result, one of the most important terms the 1980s gave Turkey was 'private life', along with all its internal contradictions. In order for a separate zone called 'private life' to be defined, it had first to be named in the public sphere, and public opinion had to be formed about it. This was one of the most important components of the great transformation of the 1980s.

Foucault had asked this question: It is said that sexuality is something kept hidden; but what if, on the contrary, it is something confessed? In post-coup Turkey – in a climate where the political opposition put their hopes in the empowering of society and glorified civil society against the state, defining society as if it were the free arena of individuals – one may put the question another way: It is said that society is something which bows to state pressure and is condemned to silence; but what if, on the contrary, it is something which names and is named? What if people are naming something in conflict with their own selves when they give the name of society to their own collective? What if the society we expect to besiege the state is something which besieges itself? What if speech, which seems the only guarantor of freedom, itself invades, encircles and conquers?

III

Weekly magazines played an important role in the formation of the new discursive politics in Turkey, particularly in the naming of sexuality. It is obvious when one glances at the cover stories and main features: naming introduces the news, images introduce the story. First something is named, its image projected, and then life stories are arranged within this supposedly familiar verbal–visual naming. In the mid-1980s, for example, two weekly magazines carried stories on bisexuals (*Nokta* as a cover story, *Yeni Gündem* as a feature); but the same image was projected in both. When I heard the word 'bisexual', what stayed in my mind was the image of two men with their backs turned, and a woman; the woman's face is visible, but not the faces of the two men.

In his *Toplumsal Değişme ve Basın* (Social Transformation and the Press), Ahmet Oktay emphasized that newspaper headlines in Turkey have acquired a character more imaginative than informative, and that the lack of verbs in headlines is related to that development. According to Oktay, one function of such verbless headlines as 'Justice in Pain' and 'A Taste of Honey for the Civil Servant' is to 'incite the reader toward the news'.[4] Verbless headlines were often used in weekly magazines in the 1980s: 'A Communist Party Till When', 'A 500-Million Swindle for Villagers', 'Beyoğlu Drenched in Blood', 'Tariqats in Parliament', 'Popular Support for Strikers', 'Fasting Leave for Soldiers.' In fact verbless headlines have functions other than to 'incite'. A name interpellates and establishes that which is fact. The verbless headline does not give us news of something in the process of change, it does not tell us about a world which contains the possibility of change; nor does it draw attention to genesis. On the contrary, it transforms a quotation taken from life into an image and reconstitutes the familiar world of speech for us every day anew. For nouns to take the place of verbs in sentences represents the state of mind corresponding to an environment of stabilization in which action is banished from life and one is condemned to facts.

A matter of style should also be mentioned here. The use in news articles of verbs in the simple present (*–iyor*) or pluperfect tense (*–mişti*) was another feature of the style pioneered by weekly magazines which gradually spread to other arenas in this period. This mode of narration had a share in the familiarization of experience as well. The verbs in sentences serve to express not only action but the point of view of the speaker. Grammar books tell us that unlike the aorist (*–ir*), which denotes unbounded, continuing activity, the simple present narrates a time the speaker can know only by dipping into it in passing. So the simple present can take the suffix of the simple past (*–iyordu*) only when the speaker has herself experienced the thing narrated. In other words, the narration of an event in the simple past includes a claim that the speaker knows everything there is to be known about the event narrated, knows it as someone who has lived it.[5] But when having experienced a thing is less important than naming it, speech always precedes anecdote, experience which can be known in its singularity; and furthermore dissolves it, reducing it to quotation. In fact what the simple past did in this case was precisely to make credible the statement of one who has observed an event from outside; it ameliorated the strangeness of the image having taken priority over the news. In other words, it gave fictionality an insider effect, ensuring that even verbless speech would narrate itself as the voice of experience. Thus by use of the simple past, the tense of experience and familiarity, the press tried to give a lived quality to its fiction; to give verbless speech the vividness of narration, as if something were in fact happening and the reporter had in fact witnessed it. This style transformed life experience into images and familiarized images as experienced things.

Another fundamental characteristic of the 1980s' climate was the interest felt in the past. But the past was defined less as a historical period apparent by virtue of its distance from the present than as an object amenable to the present fantasies and needs of today's consumers. The past was transformed into a quotation; to use Jameson's phrase, a 'pop history'[6] more representative of opinions and stereotypes than of a historical past. And this was what was achieved by the drowning of Turkey's Generation of '68, all at once, in speech. Here too are the reasons why the explosion of speech about the 1968 movement occurred not in the 1970s – which despite everything that happened then, were closer to it, not driven beyond reach by a great rupture – but in the 1980s. It was in the 1980s that the need to name the 'Generation of '68' was felt; moreover, it was the discursive politics of the 1980s which made it possible to name it. The '68 movement was reproduced within a pop history; voided of its historical burden and transformed into a spirit without content, a reception of the past easily consumed, a privileged generational ideology coloured by a call to individualism of now middle-aged, middle-class people. Because in the 1970s the history of the left was coded as the antithesis of the 1980s' discourse of individualism – and because the great majority of 1970s' leftists were not, unlike those of 1968, middle class – it could only be turned into pop by means of a 'lower' aesthetic diction, the diction named arabesk. Arabesk in Turkey was born in the 1970s; it was the naming of it that put its stamp on the process which occurred in the 1980s. Arabesk emerged in the 1980s to name not only the desire felt by provincial hordes besieging the big city to make their voices heard, to win a place in the market of images, to orient themselves in the alien big city culture, disrupt it and assimilate it, but also to name the struggle by the 'true' owners of the city to repulse foreigners, and, first and foremost, to name that foreignness.

The past always turns into something else. But here what I want to emphasize is not that the past is taken out of our hands, for the politics of prohibition does that quite well too. What was new here was that it was done not merely by silencing but by inciting to speech. Images were emptied of their historical burden and the past made a consumable quotation by means of a new discursive politics allowing a completely arbitrary language to abide in varied arenas. If the press was one pioneer of this new language in Turkey, the other was advertising. The language of advertising not only subordinated words in the service of images, it transformed the entire culture into raw material, the sum of an infinite number of quotations, to be used in the sale of commodities. It made the relationship formed with culture one of gesture and enchantment, sudden arousal and shock, a relationship of shop window display and spectacle. While tearing those who know an object asunder from those who promote it, the knowledge based on recognition from the knowledge of promotion, it encouraged a new diction that could be used in other arenas as well, a synthetic language having an arbitrary relationship to what it described, a language able to quote comfortably from the registers of conversation, journalism, technical jargon, theoretical and philosophical terms, slang, literature and politics, while remaining equally distant from all.

In a climate where experience is encircled by speech that controls, aestheticizes and names, there are still things one can do to demonstrate that there is more to language than that. If it is impossible to return experience to the history from which it has been torn, one can give that history back to experience. We can name the regime which displays itself to us as an impartial thing; we can construct its history. In Jameson's article cited above, he emphasized the need felt in this gigantic system, this divided culture encircling the subject of late capitalism, for a knowledge that would furnish the subject with a sense of place – a 'cognitive mapping'.[7] I suppose what we need to be able to do today is draw a map of the new regime of speech which condemns some knowledge to silence while drowning others in words, and also of the institutional, practical and power relationships behind it.

V

Before the general election of 1987 the journalist Ertuğrul Özkök said, surveying the campaign scene on a television programme, that social democrats in Turkey were no longer using images of 'children with flies on their faces' as they used to do; they had adopted a more 'civilized' mode of propaganda. The campaign theme worked by advertising agencies the social democrats employed for that election hammered home the point that people had been 'squeezed dry like lemons and thrown away'. It was this campaign theme Özkök took as proof that Turkey had finally become a civilized country.

Clearly the transition from 'children with flies on their faces' to 'lemons squeezed dry' does indicate a change. For the relationships which the two images set up with external reality, the modes in which they reproduce them and the references they make to the life experience they depict, are different. But before we rejoice in being civilized, we should ask what it means to reject the first and accept the second in the name of civilization; what kind of naming does this affirm? Both images aestheticize life, true. But the life experience coded by the second has been almost entirely erased. The lemon of the campaign did not bring to mind what the idiom 'squeezed like a lemon' used to express – to be used up, to lose one's vitality. The image established to express lack, poverty and exhaustion had long since created its own world, established its own familiarity. The quotation had dried up the source from which it was drawn, caused it to be forgotten, and taken its place. What the 'child with flies on his face' depicted had no importance in the new regime of speech Özkök assumed to be an instance of civilization. For the poverty which still made itself felt in those pictures, even if behind an ideological gaze, had long since become, in the new regime of speech, that ideological gaze itself; evidence of how 'primitive' left discourse was.

A newspaper article written in those years has also stayed with me. In this case it was the sociologist Nilüfer Göle discussing election results. She said that the triangle of 'state–intellectuals–the people' in Turkey had given way to one of 'government–political parties–social participation'. This change had come to symbolize a transition from the concept of 'the people' to that of 'individuals and civil society'.[8] But in the same article she also said that this transformation announced a change in the position of intellectuals too; the time of the modernist–Westernist intellectual who sought to save the people from 'ignorance and backwardness', and the leftist political intellectual who sought to save them from 'exploitation', was over. Göle based her analysis on a critique of statist left discourse, well and good; but while critiquing one error attention should be paid to how a different content has silently taken its place. Here too there is something being erased behind concepts; here too, as in the case of 'ignorance and backwardness', the term 'exploitation' has become merely the sign of an ideology; in this construct, 'exploitation' now meant nothing more than a characterization of the old leftist intellectual, an expression of his/her statism, relationship to power, and populism. Just as poverty was for Özkök evidence of leftist primitiveness, for Göle exploitation was the site where statism is located; more importantly, that's all it was. Just as when the word 'labour' evokes only a primitive or statist character now identified with the left, it is as if people no longer labour, as if they were no longer exploited, as if there were no poor people anymore.

If we are going to speak of an 1980s' climate in Turkey, it must be emphasized that this climate expressed itself first of all with a new language. To be sure, language always has an imaginative, fictive side; in every age some concepts gain importance while others fall from favour. But what was different about the 1980s was that while language dropped some terms and took up others, it succeeded in changing fundamentally our relationship to it, making viable an arbitrariness which banished familiarity, or experience, completely, and while detaching itself from reality made a fantastical diction seem authentic. The concepts of 'labour' and 'exploitation' did not only go out of fashion in the dominant discourse of the 1980s: they came to consist merely of connotation, of an ideological burden; they came to symbolize a leftism people wanted to forget as soon as possible, and a credulity identified with it. The process occurred so rapidly that words for poverty were able to acquire meanings completely different from what they had once evoked; they became mere codes for the condition of being primitive, unfashionable, or the making of a presumably un-modern demand for power, as pre-1980s' negativity. Perhaps most importantly of all, the search for truth was itself identified with naive credulity.

This arbitrariness was an important characteristic of 1980s' headlines also. Headlines now cut their ties to the world they gave news of and worked for themselves, constructing their own world. In essence they were based on wordplay or jokes which usually bore no relation to the news reported, generally onomatopoeic play on the sounds of words. It is enough to glance over a few mid-1980s headlines which first appeared in weekly news magazines and gradually spread throughout the entire print press: 'Panama'da İç Kanama'; 'Katibime Cola'lı Gömlek'; 'Türk Müziğinde Suna Kan Davası'; 'Dalyan'ın Kerataları'.[9] Names and adjectives were now organized arbitrarily, by virtue of their associations merely, quotable according to whim. What is interesting here is that this fantastical language promoted by advertising and the press, this arbitrary regime of speech, this wordplay having broken all ties to a search for the truth, was able to make itself authentic in such a short period of time and reproduce itself so quickly in so many arenas.

VI

One must speak of a great cultural rupture in Turkey today. On the one hand there is a Turkey that distances itself from poverty, from protest and from the downtrodden, a Turkey that wants to define itself as having nothing to do with such troubles. The images of privilege offered by advertising, the plenty displayed in shop windows and the 1980s' press – that entire accumulation, all of those images – succeeded in creating the impression of an ideal which everyone could achieve. As if we too, like Westerners, could pretend not to see, as if we could step over the starving people lying in the street as one does on the sidewalks of New York.

The other Turkey begins where the images end. The Turkey of losers, people deprived of the right to speech smack bang in the middle of an explosion of speech, people shut up in prisons and ruled by prohibition. The 1980s attempted to separate the world of plenty and opportunity from the world of want and impossibility, make of them two camps that never would touch, between which none could cross. Now it must be asked: Will a force reawaken to translate the opportunity of the first into the rebellion of the second? Once a culture industry transforming all into a total of images, a society ready to say yes to difference and internalize it, a regime of speech that erases completely the experiences to which concepts can give voice, has drawn us into its zone of influence, who will say that all these namings are not real? Will the knowledge pushed into the background by the regime of speech, knowledge neglected and made invisible, be able to find a less alien regime of naming for itself? In a climate where it seems that rules have been relaxed, will knowledge subject to naming even before it begins to speak be able to rise again some day?

THREE

Privation

I

WHEN WE TAKE A LOOK at Turkish newspapers from the period
we notice right away that after the 12 September 1980 coup there
seems to have been little of interest to the public but news of
'anarchy and terror' aimed at legitimizing it. The pages of *Hürriyet*
newspaper were filled almost completely by items on murders
within families. In none of those images can one find signs of
the state violence which was an ordinary fact of everyday life,
the truth of Turkey in those years. Violence became dissociated
from the state precisely when it became the state's usual practice;
as if it were a phenomenon of private life, as if the only reasons
for violence could be personal.

Censorship of the press comes to mind first of all as an explanation for this increase in images of private life; after the coup, the
press gravitated towards topics which posed less risk. But looking
back, one can find in this tendency signs of a new climate that
would put its stamp on the second half of the 1980s, and that

we don't much notice today because we are so drenched in it. True: 12 September exerted a control over the press unparalleled in recent history. But, as we have seen in the previous chapters, it also pioneered a new process; accumulation of capital in the media sector increased to an unprecedented extent after the coup. New newspapers and new weekly news magazines emerged in the marketplace, aimed at a gradually more well defined readership; magazines addressing homemakers, working women, young women, men, successful men, young professionals. In a sense, it was when the subjects of news were most restricted that the number of newspapers and magazines most sharply increased. And immediately afterwards, private television channels began broadcasting alongside the old state channels.

The restriction in certain arenas must be contemplated together with the growth in others. The sudden rise of media in Turkey was due to their extension into areas they had not tampered with before. 'Private life' was one of those arenas, and it was brought before the public eye; newspapers, magazines and private television channels created new zones of reportage for themselves to the extent they were able to encircle private life and spur expectations, arouse desires, manufacture fantasies about it – in short, to the extent they were able to invade it.

Thus the 'family tragedy' news filling the pages of papers after the coup was a harbinger of this more premeditated 'private life' journalism. But only a harbinger. For the 'family tragedy' which exposed the 'inner side' or 'backstage' of private lives had long been a classic form of sensationalist journalism in Turkey. In fact the structural transformation of media was achieved not by scandalizing private life, but on the contrary by defining it through positive suggestion, by constructing new lifestyle models, encouraging people to speak out loud about it – in short, by reinventing private life as a representable zone. Heretofore considered sacred in Turkey and therefore scandalous when exposed to public scrutiny, private life became something to be talked about, an object of confession and soul-bearing, for the first time. No longer a zone occupied by extraordinary or negative figures, famous stars, wives who killed their husbands or men who murdered their sweethearts, it became a sphere of ordinary and positive figures – politicians, businessmen, housewives, writers, everyone, great and small.

The slide of interest from the public to the private sphere which began in Turkey in the 1980s was doubtless in part coerced. Every repressive period, every constraint put upon the life of the street, the workplace, trade unions, political organizations or professional institutions, forces people to withdraw, into the home, into solitude, into the inner world. But what left its stamp on Turkey in this period was not this kind of inward turn, not a withdrawal into privacy. On the contrary, what had long been private was brought out into the open; it was transformed into news, information, images. After the 'Speaking Turkey' period, in what may be considered a short period of time, people who had once frozen before cameras and microphones, unable to put two words together as if cornered in a government office or police station, learned not only to talk on television but to speak directly about themselves; not in the name of some institution or mode of thought, but about love, sexuality, the pain of lost love, even the death of loved ones, uninhibitedly. They realized that the camera was no longer interpellating them in the formal language of institutions but personally now, in a discourse of familiarity, and that they should answer the call in the same uninhibited mode. Nowadays a man who jumps off the Bosphorus bridge and is saved through felicitous coincidence may open the gates of his inner world to a television reporter interviewing him on the spot; someone who has just lost a loved one can share his pain with a reporter and answer questions once unheard of.

There is certainly a 'private life industry' here. Once the sphere of subjectivity is besieged by instruments of mass communication, the emergence of certain professions is unavoidable. Turkey now has private-life journalists, private-life cinema, private-life novels, private-life songs; all have long since created their own languages. Yet it is impossible to attribute this entire process and its so rapid accomplishment in Turkey to an 'industry'. For it all arrived with a promise of liberation. It was as if just for a moment, people opened their realm of privacy to others, and the transformation of the private into something public filled the empty space of the public arena. If they had not found a promise of liberation in it, subjectivity would not have been so easily opened to the industry in such a short time.

So, the question is: What does the dissolution of the boundary between private and public mean for us in Turkey today? Why was it offered up to us as a promise of freedom? Who was supposed to answer the call?

II

We begin by assuming that there is a boundary, a difference between the language of the world of work, politics, contracts, newspapers and advertising on the one hand, and that of the home, friendship, love, sexuality and solitude on the other; that we are divided between them, and that they are sometimes balanced, sometimes in tension, sometimes in conflict. Furthermore, we know that this division is as old as city life. The Ancient Greeks drew a line between the *polis*, the realm of the city, and the *oikos*, the realm of the home. In Ancient Rome, *res publica* and *res privata* delineated two different presences, two different spheres of power. But it would be wrong to think that these distinctions are ancestors of the modern division. For although the division is as old as the city (*medine*) itself, which is to say as old as civilization (*medeniyet*), the forms and meanings it takes on throughout history differ. Today in the modern world we tend to link the private with nature and freedom, and the public with obligation and duty. But for the Ancient Greeks, the *oikos* was the realm of work and economy as well as the home; the home ensured reproduction. Home life meant nature, but nature was more a matter of obligation than freedom; in order to reach the realm of freedom one had to leave the *oikos* and enter the *polis*, for the *polis* was the realm of free men while the *oikos* was the realm of those deprived of freedom, those imprisoned in the realm of obligation – slaves, women and children.[1] There are traces of a similar privation in the *privatus* concept of the Ancient Romans; one meaning of the term was 'deprived of public office or rank': *privatus* defined the work a person occupying public office could perform without violating that office.[2] This sense of privation has long since been erased from the modern meaning of the term. The term 'private', with the meaning of 'intended for or restricted to the use of a particular person, group or class of persons: not freely available to the public', indicates a presence rather than a lack, not deprivation but wealth. There is a similar antinomy in Turkish between the more archaic word *mahrem*, which we still use today, and the newer term *özel hayat*. The term *mahrem* denotes both what belongs to a particular person (*harem*), and a certain privation (*haram*); the word *özel* is defined in dictionaries as 'concerning only one individual, belonging to one person'.[3]

It is within the framework of the new term *özel* that one must consider the explosion in private life which began in Turkey in the 1980s. I will dwell upon the reasons why people were so hungry for this change and experienced it as something that occurred in what may be considered a brief period of time. But it will be useful here, in order to understand the Turkish difference, to look briefly at what sort of duality the public–private division represents in bourgeois society.

III

The Latin term *res publica* signified that which belonged to society as a whole, what could not be bought and sold at market; in that sense it was identical to the power of the state, which acted in the name of all the people. But in the modern city 'public' began to describe an area formed outside the power of the state, one which came into being along with the market economy precisely by means of goods bought and sold. It was this new meaning of the public which shaped the modern private–public antinomy. As capital accumulated in cities and a distinct middle class having shared interests emerged, there came about a public space separate from the state, and a city etiquette making those interests possible; as a result of the same process there emerged a private life defined by its distance from the public. In its general outlines, this meant separation of the sphere of consumption from the sphere of production, leisure time from time spent at work, the home from the workplace, and finally the bedroom from the other rooms in the house, its concealment from strangers and acquisition of special meaning.[4] Another result of was the differentiation of the language of private life from that of public life. Thenceforth the two languages would maintain their distance, preserving their vitality by preserving the tension between them.

In *The Fall of Public Man*,[5] Richard Sennett used the term 'public' to denote societal networks formed outside the circle of family and close friends, networks which inevitably brought various social groups together independent of the direct control of the state. In this sense the focus of public life is the big city, which creates a geography where strangers can regularly meet. Sennett in any case based his discussion of public man on the opportunity which emerged in the great cities of Europe in the eighteenth century, particularly in Paris and London. A rich public life developed in these cities because the traditional social stratification had worn away and people could no longer form opinions about one another in natural ways – that is, with regard to family and ancestry. Now an etiquette was required in order to form relationships with strangers; but people were not yet settled enough, as they would be in the next century, to make distinctions of 'us' and 'them', 'insiders' and 'outsiders'. As a result of the coinciding of all these factors, the boulevards, great parks, cafés, theatres and operas where people of eighteenth-century cities went *en promenade* became sites of a lively public life which brought them together with strangers of varied social status coming into the city. But there was also a realm of privacy closed to the world of strangers which could only be defined by its distance from that public life. Sennett drew attention to the similarity between theatrical costume and street attire in societies where public life was vital. Both were different from attire worn at home; both decorated the body. In the eighteenth century, unlike today, an actor was not a more convincing Romeo if he had a legendary love life. On the contrary, the success of an actor depended on his being able to hide his true nature while on stage. People formed relationships in public in the same way, without revealing their personal histories; indeed they were able to form relationships precisely because they did not.

Sennett wrote that in the next century the balance of relationships broke down; private life was differentiated from public as the superior, richer or more authentic realm, and public life took on the inauthentic functions with which we are familiar. In the nineteenth-century industrial city, the bourgeois family was not only the site of nature; it was elevated as a refuge from the threat of the street and the severe discipline of the world of work. The banishing of children from public life and the differentiation of consort with strangers as a dangerous arena only adults could cope with was also the product of this period. Strict discipline began to be enforced in the home as a reaction to the disarray of public life; the family became the centre of emotional life and was transformed into the site of character development. The differentiation was also one of space; rich and poor neighbourhoods were separated, and neighbourhoods began to become internally homogenous. Suburbs built outside the cities meant the flight of the middle class from the squalor increasing inside the cities, from the threat of poverty and social unrest. Now an innocent private life could only be lived far from foul air, prostitutes, sickness and evil. As a secure, clean home life was distanced from the dangerous, filthy city that filled one's wallet, one of the most basic conditions for public life disappeared. Sennett pointed to the rise of privacy as public life lost its value in modern city culture and it was replaced by a more personal, yet emptier, mode of life. The transformation of the city into a homogenous economic unit, the retreat from the public world into the family as people worried about how to protect themselves, the increasingly dominant view that the family was a refuge from the public realm, of higher moral value and greater authenticity – all these were different faces of the same change. According to Sennett, there coincided in this historical moment a view that public life was a realm of inauthentic obligation or a morally reprehensible mode of life and the decline of value in actions carried out at a certain distance from the desires and needs of the self.[6]

Sennett's narrative is important because it allows us to review our assumptions about modern man with a critical eye. Today we are accustomed to speak of the inviolability of private life; but it is also quite possible to speak of the violation of the public sphere by the personal. We are inclined to speak of the repression of sexuality; but Sennett reminds us that when we rebel against sexual repression, we rebel against the societal dimension of sexuality as well. Today we tend to complain of the pressures upon private life, but when we protest against them we may be contradicting the fact that private life has a societal dimension also. We say that the instruments of public communication have destroyed privacy, but Sennett speaks of the 'despotism of privacy'. We have learned to look down our noses at objectivity, while Sennett critiques our age as 'the age of radical subjectivity'. Finally, we are inclined to believe that people have lost the desire to participate in social action, or to work together with strangers; but, according to Sennett, even this view is misleading, for it registers merely psychological states without taking into account the objective reason for the loss of participation: the decline of the public sphere itself.

Here I begin with similar questions. Why do most of us today see public life as the sum total of arid commitments merely for show? Why does experience seem meaningless to us if it is not personal? Why must we transform social phenomena into personal issues in order to make them meaningful? Why do we find meaning in political affairs only when we translate them into psychological terms? Why is the language of politics today so informal, so personal? But if we are to explain the explosion of 'private life' in Turkey after 1980, we must immediately add a more fundamental question. To what degree does the modern tension of which Sennett speaks obtain in Turkey? To what extent was the public sphere now lost to Turkey formed in the way Sennett describes? When we extricate our private life from the public, what sort of realm of obligation do we separate it from? From whom is the private hidden? Who is the stranger in the city?

IV

Yakup Kadri Karaosmanoğlu's novel *Ankara* is to my knowledge the sole urban utopia in modern Turkish literature.[7] Like most works of its genre, *Ankara* poses the fundamental question of how private and communal life can be combined in an ideal form.

62

The novel relates the intertwined stories of a newly founded city and a woman's private life. More precisely, in this book they are one and the same; everything shaping the life of the community finds its counterpart in Selma Hanım's inner world, so much so that she cannot even imagine a man outside of military uniform during the years of the National Resistance and leaves her bank manager husband to marry the war hero Colonel Hakkı Bey. But as the National Resistance spirit wanes, the marriage tie between Selma Hanım and Hakkı Bey grows slack; Hakkı Bey loses all attraction for his wife when he leaves the army and becomes a businessman. In the third, utopian part of the novel, Selma Hanım marries the writer Neşet Sabit, who has remained loyal to the spirit of National Resistance. The relationship between public and private life is unmediated; every change in public life is directly reflected in private life; each new phase in the life of the city requires Selma Hanım to find a new husband.

Clearly, the author is criticizing the new civil order established after the declaration of the Republic. Compared with the feverish environment of the National Resistance years, the new city of *alla franga* entertainments, New Year's Eve balls and tango dancing is 'false, affected, borrowed and contrived like something from a bad play'. Yakup Kadri always uses this theatre/authenticity, role/sincerity opposition when criticizing the new city. Life there transpires in a borrowed decor and people are puppets. The counterpart in private life is 'the cold family order', 'the refined marital style', whereas the soul of love, friendship and marriage is the interaction between the public and the individual. Confronted by the coldness of civic life, its aridity and falsity, one longs for 'the simple, sincere and utterly personal' life of the National

Resistance era. And so, in the third part of the novel, where the ideal city the author dreams of is described, the public realm in Ankara has assimilated private life completely. There 'all bodies so cleave together, all breaths are so mingled that every individual is divested of all personal feeling, physically as much as spiritually, and ten thousand are one and one, ten thousand.'

Although the anxieties we would expect from a novel make themselves felt here and there in *Ankara* (although Selma Hanım is sometimes tested by personal sufferings irreconcilable with community, jealousies and fears of growing old, losing her figure and the beauty of her skin), ideology always outweighs all other considerations. Personal sufferings fade into communal anxiety. Selma Hanım 'forgets herself in the community'. There is no place there for privacy because Ankara is her own home; there 'every new building is her property, every young person is her child.' There is nothing outside the public domain in this urban utopia, for the public domain has already assimilated the state, economic life and the personal. Just as work and pleasure are in themselves artificial and borrowed things, personality is in itself soulless and cold as well. Personal life is authentic to the degree that it has dissolved in the collective and been purified of passion, desire and sensuality. The most personal, most sensual moment to be experienced in Selma Hanım and Neşet Sabit's ideal relationship is described thus: 'Neşet Sabit lay his head with its jet-black hair on Selma Hanım's knees like a sacrifice and she, closing her eyes, kept on caressing the wild fringe on that young head for a long moment – an infinite, innumerable moment.' But the images of the description ('like a sacrifice', 'wild fringe') betray the fact that rather than give themselves over to such 'moments of love' behind closed doors, the two lovers will prefer to amuse themselves among the people and with the people, and in that way satisfy their desires.

Ankara is a civil servant's utopia. There is no need for privacy because the city is anyway not defined as a place which includes strangers. It is a place where 'once you've met someone, the second time you run into him you are like friends of forty years.' Yakup Kadri finds in everyone – civil servants, labourers, villagers, intellectuals – the same pioneering spirit, the same romantic spirit, the same 'feverish commitment' to the new order. The all-consuming public is moreover described in terms belonging to subjectivity. The general thrust is personal, warm and sincere, and this is reflected in the novel's style. A romantic language of privacy is the only diction the author can use to speak of politics, the life of work and the workplace. He speaks of the 'lyrical leaps in the spirits' of workers, and 'the feverish commitment' felt by everyone. The language used to describe the public is as personal, joyous and sincere as the one used for the inner world is dry and vapid.

V

In fact there was no need for strangers or privacy in utopian Ankara. In order for privacy to emerge, the ubiquitous embrace of the public would have had to relax and private life be delineated as a separate sphere alien to the life of the city. In Turkey this disengagement only began to show itself shyly in the 1950s, and in Istanbul rather than in Ankara. While the Ankara of Yakup Kadri's utopia grew, Istanbul, once the seat of the Ottoman sultanate, was forced to forget its former 'felicitous' state[8] and acquire its new identity as a big city whose streets presented their inhabitants with a true public life and the furtive excitements strangers can offer. But the utopia of Ankara had already in those years defined itself against Istanbul – the Istanbul of *gaẓino*s, bars, palaces, tea house dancing, jazz; 'the centre of business and pleasure, city of tourism, the cosmopolitan harbour'. Istanbul symbolized a public which that utopia somehow just could not internalize; an inauthentic public.

In Turkey the concept of 'the public' came to be defined within official ideology less as a domain of civil society outside the state than one which emerged under state patronage and control: the public of 'The *kamutay* was born today, it choked the sultanate away.'[9] It was not so long ago that when we heard the word 'public' in Turkey, we understood it to mean something identified with the state and, perhaps to some extent, to mean those relationships formed by way of politics. For the patronage relationships formed between different classes by way of political parties were always more important than the anonymity of the world of work and the social clubs and associations of the cities; patronage relations brought together far greater numbers of people from more walks of life. Moreover, this was true also for the 'public' of the 1970s' left, probably the only public formed without state patronage as a result of autonomous dynamics. Politics in the 1970s provided a meeting ground for people whose class backgrounds were different enough that they would not otherwise have had contact in the normal course of their lives. Political life in the 1970s brought together the wealthy and the poor, the 'cultured' and uncultured, people with different lifestyles and opportunities for advancement; a labourer could meet a young person who would in the normal course of events become a boss or supervisor; a young person who grew up in a shanty town could meet a student from a wealthy family; a villager recently arrived in the city could meet the child of an old Istanbul family – all were brought together around the shared promise of a better life. I suppose it was during those years that I most often thought it possible for the word 'public' to mean something beyond the official sense of the word, and felt we needed the term to define the ways in which strangers form relationships in an urban environment, a certain permeability offered by modern city life.

The 1970s' radical left movement succeeded in creating a public realm different from the ideal propounded by official ideology, a public realm which included strangers. But perhaps we should say it succeeded too well. The public realm which the 1970s' Turkish left extricated from the domain of the state was in its relationship to the private and personal as absolutist as the one it replaced. Rich and poor, educated and uneducated, shanty-town dweller and civil servant's child did come together on the common ground offered by the 1970s, but only by forgetting their own identities, their own roots and cultural character; and, more to the point, by behaving as if all that didn't matter. When we look back now, we can see there was an opportunity in the political environment of the 1970s. We can imagine that people could have come together without paring away the differences stemming from personal history, that they could have formed partnerships based on mutuality without surrendering to mediocrity. And perhaps this seems to us now to have been an opportunity because it has been lost. Many people who came out of the 1970s' left movement now realize that even if political action becomes independent of the state, so long as it does not enfranchise strangers it will narrow the dimensions of the private and destroy the personal utterly. But once the Generation of '68 discourse emerged in the 1980s under conditions which made it a denial of any common ground among strangers, we had to learn the reverse also: when the private is made to consist merely in itself, when everything is reduced to the randomness of a subject – of a generation, for example – all possibility for a meeting of strangers is rejected from the start. It is here one must seek the reasons why the radical left experienced 12 September not only as a political defeat but as the bankrupting of private life as well. There was no place to withdraw, no mode of speech left. Politics can only be built upon the tension between the shared and the private, the public and the personal. When a politics not constructed upon this tension is defeated, what remains is a vast emptiness.

It was in this emptiness that the great commotion which broke out over 'private life' took up residence. It presented itself as the return of what was repressed not only by the official public but by the political public of the 1970s as well, and, moreover, as its salvation. Furthermore, it used the 1970s' politicization both as its pretext and as its legacy while doing so. For privacy had already been denied, private life long since made unimportant. When the 1970s' promise of a common life was left unfulfilled, one could not return to a privacy which had lost all value. Now a private life divested of attributes began to spread into the space politics had emptied. Everything was experienced as a kind of discovery: a region long neglected, disrespected, now energized by a vision of itself as free from institutional supervision, was trying to resurface and demand its rightful place in the public realm. All these factors combined to usher Turkey into a belated period of subjectivity, of individuality, of inwardness, all the more vehement for its belatedness. Here lay the power of the 'promise of freedom': private life opened wide its gates, as if it were freedom itself, as if there were such a thing as a private life which could be offered to everyone, as if the personal could be public property. And with a speed experienced in perhaps very few societies, in a short space of time there occurred a great explosion of privatization in Turkey. But here was the dilemma also: as private life expanded into the space left empty by politics, it found itself encircled by the most public of discourses – the language of newspapers and news magazines, television and advertising. People's private lives were spoken of to an extent they never had been before, in the media of mass communication; they were named, imprisoned in speech and images.

Right here must be added the voyeurism which was another distinguishing characteristic of the times. The success of the constant stream of 1980s' 'private life' films, in which cameras wandered lingeringly through private homes, must have been due to the opportunity they afforded for satisfaction of a long-repressed hunger to 'peep' at an aestheticized private life. If we are to speak of an 1980s' 'spirit' displayed in so many different realms, from newspaper reportage to advertising slogans, from movie screens to linguistic idiom, it must be sought in this desire to peep, in its delineation as a new kind of delight, in the fact that people found a promise of freedom in peeping.

VI

I am thinking of a carpet ad which appeared in newspapers in the 1990s: 'Where "Office" and "Home" Meet'. It pictured a father playing with his son on the carpet in his office, and, further down, the slogan 'Modern Spaces'. It implied that the modern office was not a place racked with tension but, on the contrary, that it could be the place where a person feels at home, in the comfort and peace of family life. I also remember an ad from the same years for a hotel, which portrayed the hotel experience as a visit to the home of close friends or family:

> We'll have a drink at the bar before supper. I picked up some
> fresh radicchio and mallow from the market. Ali and his wife are
> coming as well. We'll have drinks on the terrace listening to music
> at midnight. Could we ever send you away at such an hour? You'll
> spend the night with us.

This was the other side of the same process. Not only was the language of private life publicized, public language was privatized as well. In a sense, 'outer' began to behave like 'inner'. In want ads, advertising slogans, television news programmes there was a strange interpenetration of the private and the public, the emotional and the political; employment ads began to seem like personal ads. The formal language once characteristic of such listings was replaced by a sincere, personal, breezy diction. Businesses defined prospective employees not as workers who would be responsible for a given task but as people who would conform to a certain lifestyle, sharing a private life with their employers and fellow workers; they called upon them to bring their smiling good cheer, their uniqueness, and their passion for work to the job. In news reporting, even though objectivity and impartiality continued to be basic principles of journalistic discourse, old-style objective reporting was replaced by 'real life stories of people like us', 'tragic tales and portraits from daily life', incredible family dramas and 'dramatic tales'. Not only the contents of news reports, but all the discourse that makes news news, from syntax to montage, from headlines to photographs, adopted a style in imitation of literature, reporting an event as a personal story experienced by a particular subject which had news value in that sense. As headlines became personal messages, relying more and more upon wordplay and literary references ('A Jazz Night's Dream', 'The Misery of Philosophy', 'The Unbearable Lightness of Traffic'), the line between reality and fiction, journalism and literature, objectivity and subjectivity began to be obscured. The depersonalized, official style formerly used by news announcers gave way to one emphasizing personality, giving the impression that the announcer was at least as important as what he or she reported, if not more so. Announcers no longer derived their authority from the news they reported, their faces expressionless as they read texts presumed impartial in as flat a tone as possible; their authority now derived from their personal credibility and sincerity.[10] We were confronted by a new realm defining itself by its distance from the formality of the TRT,[11] a realm populated by a class of people who did not convey the news, but themselves created the agenda, sharing their feelings about it with viewers; who offered us a personal story to be shared, rather than passing on an account of events; who did not speak for any institution; who were themselves as important as the news they presented. We now loved or hated the announcer, not the institution behind the scenes, not the news network or societal system which transformed the news into that news.

That is how the new newspapers, news magazines, private television channels, private radio stations, and advertising agencies took the initiative in the formation of Turkey's new public language. A new public sphere outside of the language of General Staff pronouncements, cabinet decisions, memorandums and court proceedings. A new public which found its most conspicuous expression in the style of talk-show hosts chatting on television screens before people they did not know, with guests they also in fact barely knew, as if chatting with close friends in their own home; raunchy radio announcers who bluntly exposed their own personal lives; breezy politicians who addressed voters as if they were beloved friends rather than citizens concerned with class interests, institutional conflicts and economic programmes; a new public mouthing the language of family, faith and love.

VII

I have said that utopian Ankara defined itself against Istanbul, centre of business and entertainment. But while utopian Ankara lost its credibility, Istanbul in the 1980s became the symbol of another modernization with its five-star hotels, huge shopping malls and office towers, its stock market and giant advertising billboards: a utopia of business independent of the state, a utopia of the ideal of unlimited consumerism and the free circulation of money.

But I also said above that by 'public' (*kamu*) we may mean something other than merely the official parliament (*Kamutay*), or the free circulation of capital; that we have need of this concept to define the kinds of common ground where strangers may relate within the life of the city. If that is the case, then we should ask: What is the place of the stranger in this liberal utopia promising freedom? Ankara defined the stranger as a burden to be thrown off. Alright then, does the utopia of Istanbul really define the stranger in the city as a stranger? If so, how?

In order to answer these questions we must discuss the processes transforming the life of the city, the operations making it impossible for different classes to meet in the city, the urban planning which resettles rich and poor so that they will not come into contact, the gated communities, private schools and private clubs. The 'great transformation' of Turkey which began in the 1980s has long since been accomplished: any common ground where people of different classes might meet in the big cities is almost completely gone, especially in Istanbul. True, the replacement of ethnically based neighbourhoods by class-based neighbourhoods is nothing new, and the history of the separation of rich, middle-class and poor districts goes back to ancient times.[12] What differentiates the transformation of the 1980s is as much the sweeping away of shared space, in which people of different classes may form relationships, as it is the complete separation of wealthy and poor neighbourhoods. Now it is not only the neighbourhoods of rich and poor that are separated but also their shopping centres, educational institutions and places of leisure. In this new public there will never again be relationships between those who attend the Istanbul Festival and those who go to the Gülhane Festival, those who go to Fame City and those who go to neighbourhood amusement parks, those who shop at Galleria Ataköy and those who shop at Beşiktaş Market, or those who shop at Akmerkez and those who shop in Mahmutpaşa; those who buy things and those who just gaze at shop windows. Many parts of the city have already been abandoned to the poor, while the rich have withdrawn into gated communities within the city where they will never even see them.

This urban differentiation did not occur without leaving its marks on the cultural sphere. One of the complaints most often voiced since the 1980s is the invasion of the big cities by rural migrants. There had been shanty towns in the big cities for some time, but the 'loss' of Istanbul came to be voiced most often then, when the building of shanty towns began to slow down. There was arabesk music in the 1970s, but people only began to complain about it in the 1980s; arabesk became the name not only of a style of music alien to the old residents of the city but whatever was 'uncultured'. It was also recently that membership of the 'Generation of '68' became an ideology of generation-differentiating individuals, most of whom have joined the administrative classes. All of these developments indicate that the common ground which once allowed for interpenetration among classes, professions and generations has been wiped out, that the lines separating strangers have become stronger than ever before, and the city far more polarized.

It is in this sense also that the lost opportunity of the 1970s' 'public' of the left was very important. For as that opportunity was being lost, as the people who once came together around the promise of a shared life returned to the positions defined by their class – as one became a bank manager and another a janitor at the same bank, as one took up a position of leadership while another sank into unemployment – it was not only that shared promise but the idea of anything shared with strangers that was lost as well. Now most of the news on television is bad news; it informs us of a world filled with dangerous strangers, a world dominated by danger, terrorism, perversion and scandal. The strangers who live in the same city with us now have a place on television screens only to the degree that they are an 'affliction'. Shanty towns, villagers and rural folk, workers, civil servants and students are represented on television screens only when they pour into the streets, clash with the police, use drugs, run amuck, when they die in accidents – it is only by these images that they are represented. News bulletins now confront us with those ostracized by society only when they constitute a threat. While the discourse of reporting today, with its continuous stream of bad news and images reminiscent of horror films, transforms the reporter into a detective and the news announcer into a judge, it has already transformed the public sphere into a realm of calamity from the very start. The only real news conveyed to us is that evil is outside and we are inside, that our private world is always safer than the dangerous, eerie public realm where death roams free.

We have come from the fiction of Ankara, where strangers did not exist, to the fiction of global Istanbul where the stranger is perceived as a threat. But we can now also see the limitations of the promise. The distinction between private and public, the border between 'inner' and 'outer', has been worn away in Turkey. Which has lost more in the process – the public which imposes itself as something 'inner', or the private which has completely lost its 'outer' – time will tell. The sphere of subjectivity has never been so besieged by the public, and others have never promised so little.

VIII

A last word, or rather a memory of mine. In Turkey the wall between the middle-class sitting room and the guest room was torn down long ago. The new space called a salon was supposed to combine the two functions; it would serve both as the place where the inhabitants of the home gathered to sit and as the place where guests would be entertained. This can be interpreted as the collapse of the formality used with strangers, and the opening of the doors of privacy to those coming from outside; or as the elimination of guests all together. When I consider how the spatial alteration transformed our life in my childhood, it occurs to me that my mother became more irritable in the new organization of our home. There was a simple reason: the salon had always to be kept neat for guests who might swoop in at any time. That is why I recall our early life with a salon as a life spent on tenterhooks. When the doorbell rang there would be a race towards the private parts of the house, a hurried tidying up, and the front door would be opened only after some time. When it became clear that it was only the building caretaker at the door, those waiting in the long corridors between the salon and the other parts of the house would get the news that the danger had been warded off.

I recorded the guest room in my memory as a cold, functionless region. As a child it wasn't clear to me why my older sister and I slept in the sitting room while the people called guests, who rarely visited the house, had a separate room. As it turned out, that cold but always well-ordered space, and that first frenzy later during the change to salon life, indicated a transitional moment. Let there be no misunderstanding: I am not trying to say that strangers were made much of, that guests were often welcomed in the homes with guest rooms of my childhood. On the contrary, the doors to those rooms, with their dusty, little-used sideboards, their artificial flowers in crystal vases and silver candy dishes awaiting guests, were always closed; they cried out their unlivedness to those who opened their doors; they were little more than places for children to hide. They were emptied signs. Yet when I consider the informal culture of today, I think, perhaps because it gives me a sense of distance, that an interior can only develop if there is an exterior; I call to mind those people who did not live their lives by that truth but were willing to sacrifice a room to it. And that cold emptiness which has long since lost its function, but they could not do without.

FOUR

The Return of the Repressed

I

FREDRIC JAMESON wrote in his 'Periodizing the 60s' that the 1960s' cultural-political environment of the First World had its origins in the Third World. The loss of African colonies by England and France and the emergence of new Third World forms of resistance were its harbingers. The period began with the First World's discovery of 'natives' beyond its borders, its discovery that there was a Third World 'out there'. This initial discovery led to another: as the First World became aware of the peoples of Ghana, Congo, sub-Saharan Africa and Algeria, it discovered the 'natives' and 'third worlds' within its own borders; its own internally colonized peoples, its own 'minorities', its women, its blacks, homosexuals and marginals.[1]

There was a similar double discovery at the centre of the recent cultural transformation in Turkey. Turkey discovered its own periphery, its own 'third world', its own 'natives'. It was

78

forced to discover the native-born it had pushed from the centre, condemned to silence, provincialized – above all the Kurds. But there was more; Turkey also discovered parts of its own self it had repressed to become modern – its Islamic face, its Easternness, its hinterland which would return as 'low culture'. Those who had not yet had the chance to express themselves culturally – 'the rural', 'the peripheral', 'minorities', most of all the Kurdish minority – broke their silence in the gigantic explosion of speech in the 1980s. But there was more still: those relegated to the private realm also began to speak; for the first time women and homosexuals spoke out forcefully, in public, for themselves. It was during those years that Turkey discovered sexuality, something which had never quite been visible in its modern identity. Sexuality became one of the most popular topics in the expanding media as newly proliferating newspapers and weekly news magazines sought to increase their circulation; sexuality was spoken of with a hunger never felt before, a burning desire to confess, which derived its raging energy from its enforced belatedness. The insistent naming of the sphere called 'private life', and its instant publicization, were phenomena of the same years. In the wake of all these simultaneous explosions Turkey entered a period of cultural dissolution which was praised by some as cultural pluralization and disparaged by others as a 'rural invasion', a 'cultural degeneration' that took the particular form of 'the return of religion' and in fact harboured several dynamics, positive and negative, all at once. In the phrase defined by Freud as a basic concept of metapsychology, it was 'the return of the repressed', with all the violence that implies.

II

At first glance the reason for the cultural pluralization of the 1980s in Turkey appeared to be the brutal suppression of the powerful 1970s' socialist movement by the 12 September 1980 coup. When the socialist movement lost its place as a focal point of opposition, it also lost its ability to hold within itself, as part of its own grand narrative, the energies it had set in motion. Political opposition naturally slid into more cultural, more private realms when the left grand narrative lost its former power. But rather than attribute the cultural fragmentation of that period to the defeat of the left, we may find a more accurate explanation for these two changes by analysing the cultural transformation which prepared the conditions for both. The fundamental cause of cultural fragmentation was the unravelling of modern identity as it had been constructed for Turkish society by the founding Republican ideology known as Kemalism.[2] Kemalist ideology lost the ability it once possessed to hold differing identities together, whether by way of persuasion or force; in other words, it lost its promise of modernity, its competency in the realm of modernity, its monopoly on modernity. Not only those silenced within the left opposition, or vocal only to the extent they conformed to its grand narrative, all those who had not been able to speak within the modernizing project, all of the content Turkey had left out while constructing its modern culture and pushed to the margins of modern identity – yes the Kurds, but also Islamists, also women, also homosexuals – now returned as speaking subjects with voices of their own.

This transformation, fragmenting and pluralizing culture at the same time, made itself felt in the second half of the 1980s in several spheres at once, but it came to the fore as an explosion of 'low' or 'rural' culture in particular. Its most striking expression was the increased visibility in the cultural marketplace of content formerly disparaged as 'rural', above all the spread of arabesk music in big cities. Certainly there was a role played by the internal migration of rural populations to the big cities and the ruralization of the big cities thereby. But the flight to big cities may be traced as far back as the 1960s; the roots of arabesk music lie in the late 1960s and early 1970s. I describe the 1980s' transformation as an 'explosion' not only because the visibility of the rural in the cultural marketplace increased, but because that visibility coincided with the effort of the masses to put forth cultural identities unmediated by a grand political narrative, to search for a cultural identity not shaped by a shared political language, and because this quest found an appropriate ground in the cultural marketplace of the 1980s. I insist on the word 'explosion' here; for the sudden discharge of energy during that time included what the Kemalist modernizing project itself could not contain: a demand, a protest against the division of labour between the masters of culture and the masses – ordinary life's rebellion against the elitist language working to overcome it, in a sense ordinary life's demand to be culturalized – a demand by the local to express itself more forcefully in the cultural marketplace. Experiences, identities, the peripheral buried there, which had been able to exist within modern cultural identities only in repressed form, really did return in the 1980s with a giant bang. At the root of the arabesk explosion, and many other related phenomena as well – the attention the media showered upon cultural or religious minorities, not only Kurds but Circassians, Gypsies and Alevis; the interest taken in the novelist Latife Tekin,

who came from outside the literary mainstream and preferred to
see herself not as a novelist but as a spokeswoman for repressed
experience, the 'murmur' of poverty; the emergence of a 'prison
literature' also outside the literary mainstream – there was a role
played also by the demand of a deprivation no political or literary
discourse had ever been able to contain to speak for itself.

But I want to emphasize again that I am talking about 'natives' within. Turkey's great transformation involved not only a
discovery of 'low culture', but of contents 'high culture' had for
long years pushed down and repressed within itself in order to be
'high', repressed for the sake of being modern, Western and elite.
The market brought liberty not only to the masses predestined
for 'low culture' but to the elites who represented Kemalism as
well. For the 'high' of Kemalism required it to represent more
then itself, to act in the name of the entire society, to represent
a shared modern identity. This imperative exerted pressure upon
the elites themselves as well as forcing them to exert pressure
upon the masses. To elevate oneself to the position of society's
'mind', to stand at the ready to represent others, was something
based at least in this case not only on the power to do so but on
an ideal of duty and service, and required the elites to renounce
everything which might threaten the demands of the modern
identity. It was in this sense that the 1980s gave high culture a
sort of liberty also, a freedom to abandon its supremacy, to act
in its own name and represent itself alone. The liberal politics of
the Motherland Party, which came to power in the 1983 elections
charged with the task of ensuring that Turkey swiftly take its
place within global capitalism, indicated not only a relative liberty
for what Kemalism had repressed but the lifting of the privation

high culture had been forced to tolerate in order to be high. And that is also why the repressive period of the 1980s came into being with a promise of freedom both for low culture and for the elites themselves. It personified the return of the high-handed elites' own rural-ness, own native-ness, own 'low'-ness, an awareness that all of this could very well coexist with capitalism, that one did not have to be part of the 'high culture' to have money and power, that one did not have to be trained in modernity to be elite. In fact it is partly here that the reasons for the summoning power of both the liberal Motherland Party of the 1980s and the Islamist-liberal Justice and Development Party of the 2000s should be sought.

There was a cultural counterpart to this political transformation. Among the factors contributing to the rise of İbrahim Tatlıses, the Arabesk King who no longer felt the need to hide a Kurdish accent despised as 'broken' pronunciation, there was not only the desire of Kurds to express their cultural identity in the big city, not only the desire of rural populations to grasp the opportunities of the big city, but also the desire of older urban populations, no longer afraid of being unmodern, no longer ashamed of their rural roots, to own up to what they had been forced to repress in order to be urban. In Tatlıses's songs the rural discovered an urban identity for itself, but the urban also discovered the rural within itself, the rural it had repressed in order to be Western. It is here that one must seek the reasons why the 1980s' arabesk explosion took everyone, Turk and Kurd, under its spell, and why it spread without respect to social class. The rural populations pushed out of modern culture now grasped the opportunities the market offered and, to the extent they were able to turn their ruralness to advantage in the marketplace, began to speak freely without fear of being condemned as uncultured. There is hardly need to say that the entire process was accompanied by an explosion of desire. A society trained so long in the consciousness of duty, morality of service and renunciation finally found in the 1980s an opportunity to express desires it had been forced to postpone for so long. The old culture based on thrift, not only with money but with desire, gave way to a culture of desire; a new culture encouraging appetite and whim which summoned the people to instant gratification.

But one must see in this return the simultaneous operation of two trends at once. First, as the cultural marketplace in Turkey expanded, the rapid accumulation of cultural capital was fed by the rapid plunder of the local. That is what gave the transformation an aspect understandable through such concepts as 'mass culture' and 'culture industry'; in other words, it was constructed, incited into being. Still, these concepts are not sufficient to explain the energy released. For whenever we speak of incitement we must speak also of repressed desire, or ostracization, and resentment. If lives long deprived of the world of opportunity known as culture embark upon a search for cultural identity without obedience to an elite language, if energies forced to obey the language of modernizing political projects are able stake their own claim in the realm of culture, it is because they once really were repressed, because they once really were ostracized from modern culture. It was to these ostracized contents that the liberal market of the 1980s gave the opportunity which the modernizing project of Kemalism had not, the opportunity to modernize in some sense, or rather to join the modern world without modernizing at all. It gave them the opportunities of the big city, the world of publishing, the cassette market, the world of images and display, the entertainment sector – of the public sphere rather than just the neighbourhood, of the synthesizer as well as the saz lute. It gave them the opportunity finally to satisfy the cultural hunger they had been forced by modernity's repression for long years to suppress, the opportunity to be visible in the public sphere, to put their own symbolic language into circulation, and (at least for the stars of the rural populations) to be rich. This, then, was why the repressive period of the 1980s, despite all the violence of the prisons and censorship of the press, was able to present itself with a promise of liberation, to call itself into being as a period of freedom.

If one of two fundamental elements determining the cultural climate of the 1980s in Turkey was repression, the other was the return to the cultural marketplace of the rural, which had been left out of the modern cultural identity. When I refer to 'the rural' here I mean not only what was outside of the big cities but all the experiences society left out in order to become modern. The 1980s in Turkey symbolized a promise of freedom for what had been pushed out of modern cultural codes, the rural, which participated in those codes only as a negativity. For the 1980s gave it the hope that it could break free of the repressive costume sewn for it by Kemalism's modern identity, the hope that it could join in the market without losing its own identity.

III

In describing the cultural climate which came over Turkey in the 1980s I have had recourse to the notion of 'the return of the repressed'. I have insisted on using it for two reasons. First, in order to register the violence with which contents once ostracized from modern culture, deprived of the right to expression, had been silenced. Second, in order to demonstrate the unavoidable effects this violence had on new cultural developments, the unstoppable return evident there, and how that cultural return has necessarily affected the ongoing struggle in today's cultural sphere. But this is not without pitfalls. The return of the repressed gives us hope; we suppose that what has returned will finally be able to get what it has been begrudged, and even that once having returned, it will be able to speak not only for its own deprivation but for that of others as well. But here is the trap: the repressed never returns as the repressed thing it was, as pure content emerging suddenly after a long silence; it does not wait there, unchanging, to be discovered, or return as pure destructive energy now demanding the share once seized from its grasp. On the contrary, it returns as something shaped by the needs of the site to which it returns, always reconstructed in different forms, open to new projects and manoeuvres, reformed according to the demands of the market or 'world politics', vulnerable to relationships of power and interest. That is why what was repressed in the past is now a realm of constant struggle. Furthermore, the repressed was in fact never simply repressed; nor does it in fact ever return, not exactly. The rural that returns is not in fact the rural once repressed; nor is the religion which returns in fact the religion once repressed. Turkey's recent past is important not only because it shows how the repressed may return, but also because it allows us to see that the relationship between what was repressed and what has returned is more complex than we suppose, that the

assault of repressed desire may not always result in freedom for
individuals or societies, and, perhaps most importantly of all, that
to a great extent this is always how liberalism works anyway. The
most striking example in Turkey today is the return of religion.
The religion Kemalism repressed has returned; but the religion
returned is not the religion repressed. It is a religion locked onto
its target with the energy of victimhood, empowered to the extent
it is able to set in motion the energy of resentment, and joined to
capitalism thanks to that power. Who can assert, in the face of
the entire discourse of victimhood used by the Islamist faction,
that this religion is the faith once ostracized in Turkey? Who can
say that the arabesk music now blasting away on television is the
mournful folk music of old? Who can claim that the 'Emperor'
İbrahim Tatlıses of savvy television specials is the voice of the
silenced Kurd? Who can say that the explosion of sexuality in the
1980s was the long-awaited liberation of repressed delight? Who
can assert that 'the local' now joining the world marketplace is
the ostracized 'local' of old?

Yes, things are returning, but they have long since become
something else. For what makes their return possible is the
market. It is here that the difference between Kemalism and
liberalism must be sought. However crude, even hypocritical,
the repression imposed on the rural by Kemalism was, it always
bore a promise, a promise of modernization, of civilization.
But compared to what had been repressed, what returned in
the 1980s was much more aware – or sly; it was not going to
be fooled by promises anymore. The invisible repression of
the market, unlike those ideologies which forever postpone
gratification of desire to some time in the future, also conceals

the truth that it can never in fact be gratified. And so the desire seeming to bear the promise of liberation when repressed may renounce all promise it bears and play itself out as insolence when it returns.

IV

Jean-François Lyotard found a promise of liberation in the cultural fragmentation that ensued as the grand narratives lost their credibility. Yet he himself best described how that fragmentation was intertwined with consumer society:

> Eclecticism is the degree zero of contemporary general culture: one listens to reggae, watches a western, eats McDonald's food for lunch and local cuisine for dinner, wears Paris perfume in Tokyo and 'retro' clothes in Hong Kong; knowledge is a matter for TV games. It is easy to find a public for eclectic works.[3]

These words are important not only because they describe the new cultural condition so well but also because they indicate the limits in this world of the cultural pluralism which emerged as the grand narratives lost their credibility. And, perhaps more importantly, because they show that without a critique of capital, Lyotard's critique of the hegemony of grand narratives remains merely a spectator as smaller narratives diversify in yet another invisible grand narrative, that of the market. Much can be hoped for from 'global culture'; but as long as the fundamental dynamic of that culture is the market, neither reggae nor Turkish literature nor Kurdish poetry nor Gypsy music will be more than new commodities for international capital, new ornaments for the global city. As long as the cultural pluralism which has emerged with the loss of a centre remains an aestheticization of daily life, it will be nothing more than the freedom to consume in a world capitalism has made polycentric.

The promise borne by the repressed was built upon a negative, compensatory image which had no basis in reality. But when the repressed returns, its surrender to the conditions of its return is absolute. It stands as if bewitched before the surface of an infinite now, allowing neither dream nor negativity to spoil its pleasure. Can the return of the repressed, or the still yet repressed, or something else, now bear realistic promise? Let us keep our hope, but ask:

The repressed is returning, but as what? More importantly, where is it returning to?

FIVE

Me Too

CULTURAL IMAGES, like human beings, can only be understood when their lives are over, when the light they have shed over their surroundings is on the wane; they illuminate only when their promise is as exhausted as their potential, when the hopes tied to them have drifted away and others have taken their place. So it was with the indisputable Arabesk King Orhan Gencebay, 'big brother' to lost souls. Gencebay became the voice of the defeated with his movies and his records, starting with the very first in 1968, 'Console Me'. The voice of loners, rejected lovers, the forlorn and – experience shut out from the cultural codes of the Republic – the rural unable to make itself heard.

Throughout the 1970s Orhan Gencebay sang the same song in a piercing wail cracked by tears. We were not used to hearing a grown man break down and cry. He told of love over before it began, bad luck and trouble, trials that never end. Lovers fated not to meet till Judgement Day, long years spent in frustrated longing. Life as pain and trial was his constant theme. His was the discourse of the lover obsessed with an image so far out of reach it could never be attained, the lover crippled by love. It was always the same story. The girl faithless, distant, unreachable; the man a plaything in her hands, forlorn but honourable. The voice was always the same voice: desperately sincere, shockingly dramatic, desire made absolute in the knowledge it would never be satisfied.

But Gencebay's songs drifted away from the massive audience that once saw itself in them; it has been a long time since his music echoed the sounds of the street. Now we can speak of him as a hero whose story has come to an end. The halo around his name has faded away and he can now illuminate more than himself; he can shed light on the recent history of Turkey.

II

When I first listened to Gencebay in the 1970s that moaning, burning, sighing man's voice seemed to me almost obscene. There must have been many like me, city-dwellers who set great store by an awakened consciousness, who felt something like embarrassment at those weird songs with their frisky beat and desperate message, that keening whine borne aloft on soaring strings, that obvious pleasure in picking away at incurable wounds of love. I suppose what I saw in that public display of burning want, that broken male figure who played the condemned man seeking honour in wretchedness itself, that beggar's sincerity veering towards the banal, was uncontrolled, exaggerated, overblown desire.

The 1970s in Turkey were years when private life was not exposed in public, when it was considered unbecoming to moan and whine like that, shouting one's pain in love out loud. But Gencebay intertwined the private with the public and made of love a metaphor for tyranny. Not only that, he used the lover's discourse to complain of social oppression. Moreover, he summoned people not to overcome their bitter fate, but actually to take pleasure in it; not to overcome their pathetic circumstances but settle down into them and make a pastime of the unrequited love whose tale he told in almost every song he sang. That is why all his songs had to seem indecent to anyone who believed the black fate of the oppressed could be transcended through cultural enlightenment, transformed through political training and solidarity. And they did: in those years many people like myself heard Orhan Gencebay as the undisciplined cry of unbridled desire, the voice of the vagabond rural. Those anguished songs made us think of pastures in India or deserts in Egypt; although fiction, they seemed to insist stubbornly on an Oriental sense of victimhood, a vagabond discourse for those with no share in this world, the bricolage image of a luckless adolescent.

Twenty-odd years hence, the cultural environment which made Gencebay so important has changed along with many other things in Turkey. Today's climate is filled with desire, and when I look back, what I see in Gencebay's songs is less wild abandon than restraint. For although he constantly sang of desire, he preached repression. He told his audience they were beaten from the start in the game of desire, but there was pleasure to be had in the tension between desire and satisfaction, that a spiritual energy could be derived from frustration itself. I said that he made of love a metaphor of tyranny. But Gencebay also told his audience there was pleasure to be had in the tension created when a cry raised against tyranny cannot find its mark, pleasure to be had in being forlorn. He was saying, 'I have rights too', but, rather than insist he be given what he deserved, also saying, 'I don't want your charity'. He sang about 'taking pleasure in pain', 'being addicted to pain', 'longing for the pain of love'.

In his popular songs of the 1970s Orhan Gencebay called to the distraught new urban classes – the rural populations pouring in to become new city-dwellers, but also long-time residents who could not quite find a place for themselves in a big city which constantly fanned the flames of desire, in a game of desire where the city was personified by woman; he called upon them to withdraw. He called on them to speak in reproach rather than desire; to take up residence in dissatisfaction, in heartache, in being out of place; he invited them to desire love itself, not the one they loved; not what they desired but desire itself. He used the language of faith to give meaning to their condition in the city as a people who could not get their way, who were doomed to be out of place, always at an unbridgeable distance from the bounties of this world, always seen to be at fault in an alien world (in one song he consoled his audience: 'No God's servant is perfect'); he offered terms of 'self-sacrifice', 'forbearance', 'resignation'. I say restraint because, above all, Gencebay offered a strangerhood based on renunciation ('give up, O my heart!') and patience ('forbear, O my heart, forbear!'). True, there was also a wish for a community of sufferers: 'lovers understand how a lover feels', 'come and be with us', 'you're one of us too'; but Gencebay made it completely clear from the start that it was in reconciling oneself to lack, 'embracing a stone', that the power of belonging lay.

At first glance at least, Gencebay's diction of defeat seems the antithesis of the triumphant left discourse of the 1970s, based in the expectation that suffering would be transcended sooner or later through a revolution that would change everything. But only at first glance; for when one looks a bit closer, it may well be that Gencebay's discourse had somehow already internalized the defeat the left would eventually suffer, and that his popularity in the 1970s was related to that of the left. Not because he echoed the left in speaking of 'the law of survival', or of situations in which a man could not determine his own fate, or said that some people were not allowed the right to live in this world. And not because he said 'Someday we too will surely see that glorious tomorrow.' What related his discourse to that of the left was the way he spoke in absolutes. In his songs there was a world of categorical opposites also; friend and foe, true and false, sin and merit, longing and bliss all had sharp outlines. Here, also, desire took its power from the fact that the object of desire was absolutely unobtainable, while the one who desired was absolutely honourable. Here, also, the discourse of love was calibrated for a happiness to be attained only in the distant future; the lover has invested all of his emotional energy in a beloved he will join only on Judgement Day. Lines like 'I died while being born', 'my flesh was kneaded with pain to last a whole life long', 'O God, create me over again', and 'Let this world sink', projected an asceticism which had completely turned its back on the world. Moreover, there was a demand for justice which also echoed left discourse. Orhan Gencebay was the 'big brother' defending the rights of the family against an unjust father. Like most who joined the 1970s' left movement, he was the child of a civil servant but spoke in the name of the poor. He was well fed, but gave voice to the suffering of the hungry. He was from the city, but interpreted the trials of those who could not find their way there. He spoke of desire, but like all who defend the rights of others, and so necessarily exalt themselves to the position of 'the mind', he had recourse to the terminology of renunciation. Like all big-brother candidates for power, he too had to postpone his own desires. For now he seemed to say, 'I'm a wretch if I ask anything for myself!'

Orhan Gencebay owed his popularity in the 1970s to the fact that he internalized two apparently antithetical qualities. He projected the mutiny on the streets, his wailing tone giving victimhood a public voice, and did so by violating the customary sensibility of Turkish music. But he was also taking a step back, into traditional sensibility, into a religious discourse and a sober stance; he was deliberately measured, a gentleman, well mannered. He was a star at a time when desire was expressed not in a discourse of freedom, but on the contrary one of renunciation; when desire was voiced not by wanting more, but on the contrary by withdrawal.[1] There was a similar dichotomy in his shuttling back and forth between traditionalism and modernity. But we should not be misled by the religious discourse of his songs or the Majnun figure he played in a series of 1970s' films. Gencebay offered people who remained on the margins of modern life a way to cope with the modern condition, with the pumped-up desires of the big city. It was a modern bargain to the extent that he recommended they cope with the pains of modernization by turning the pain itself into a source of pleasure. It is here that his restraint has meaning. In the face of the explosion to which overstimulation in alien lands would lead, Gencebay proposed withdrawal.

It is not only because he has aged that his recordings are now considered classics and he is promoted from defiant 'big brother' to respectable 'Papa Orhan', but because the image he constructed with his songs, his look, and his films of the old romance hero Majnun mad for his beloved Leyla are now too slow and bulky to answer the spiritual needs of this society anymore.

III

The 1980s' cultural transformation which presented itself to us as an explosion of sounds, words and images, but also of desire, brought about the narrative explaining it as well. The desire kept repressed for so long – in the words of one of the recent countless songs speaking of the flesh, of need, of desire: 'my naked, unlived desires' – had finally reached the point of explosion. A society trained for so long in consciousness of duty, discipline and the morality of service had finally found the opportunity to express the wishes it had for so long been forced to defer. The old culture based on austerity in desire gave way to a culture of desire calling all to instant gratification.

The narrative is correct where it indicates that in the cultural transformation of the 1980s, contents Turkish society had shunned in order to become modern – yes, the repressed rural, but also repressed sexuality – met up with the opportunities of the big city and found freer expression within confines determined by the market. True, Turkey's repressed voices returned in the voice of Orhan Gencebay, but patience and renunciation were still at the core of his songs. Gencebay emphasized the impossible space between desire and satisfaction, counselling resignation, and so could not have been the star of the new era. Only a voice even more rural, and fleshier, and hungrier, could speak for the new era's desire. In the 1980s and 1990s Gencebay gave up his throne to a Kurd who had learned in foreign lands to rely on himself, who was spellbound by his own capacity to love ('O God, O God, this is the way to love') as much as by his own 'broken' accent, who wasted no time advancing on his target ('Let me wrap myself around you'), whose songs called out not to some distant, unattainable beloved but a real, named woman ('Emine, oh my, oh my'), and who rose from construction worker to Arabesk King: İbrahim Tatlıses. The deprived stepbrother forced for so long to take refuge in a big brother's justice – crushed under his big brother's desire, honour and weight – at last cried out: 'Me too!'

'Me Too': this *türkü* folk song by İbrahim Tatlıses was soon on everyone's lips, rich and poor, Turk and Kurd. It was so popular not only because it dramatized Tatlıses's personal journey from deprivation to opportunity, but because it gave voice to an entire society's wish to be free of a renunciation which now seemed merely a burden. İbrahim Tatlıses was so important because he was able to say something that could well pass through the mind of anyone who saw others better off, and sing it before all in a tone at once brazen and puckish, more than willing to play the role of little 'hick' brother if it allowed him to take up the throne left empty by 'big brother' Orhan. And so all of Turkey's children who were sick of playing the role of extra in a big brother's conscience loved İbrahim Tatlıses. Thanks to his songs, they learned to stick out their chests when they talked, to demand a share in the bounties of this world they'd had to turn their backs on, to make their own voices heard without the help of a deep-voiced older brother who always put on the brakes in the end, even if he wept and wailed while he did so. As Orhan Gencebay's star faded, Tatlıses's shone the more brightly, along with that of an audience too impatient for unrequited love, unattainable women and trials suffered a life long for the sake of one hope; listeners unwilling to put off the pleasures to be had in this world for the sake of far-off promises, and inclined to admire neither Majnun nor the dervish life.

Yet there is a side to this narrative which may be misunderstood, and has been in part misstated. However much the process that began in the 1980s presented itself to us as repressed desire finally out in the open, in fact here it was a matter not of progress towards desire from lack but of a process which transformed the dynamic of desire. So it would be more precise to say that in the new 'Me Too' climate the absolute desire which had in the past forged single desires into a totalizing narrative dissolved; the elements compounded in it became unbound. Gone was the narrative defining desire by the unqualified obstacle before it, thus imbuing it with a totalizing structure which transformed single desires into one great cultural demand, one all-out declaration of defiance ('Let this world sink', Gencebay sang). Single wishes, now no longer parts of a totalizing desire, could parade blithely in public, seeking out more concrete, realizable targets for the short term and, now with the luxury of representing only themselves, demand to be satisfied at once. The dignity which once accompanied desire suddenly lost all meaning.

The difference is obvious when we compare Gencebay's and Tatlıses's songs. One makes his investment in the non-coincidence of desire and gratification, trying to produce pleasure out of the distance between them. The other, on the contrary, plainly demands instant gratification, both with his songs and his public persona, however much he may complain of sorrow and heartbreak. One derives his energy from the fact that he is not given what he wants, and never will be in this world anyway. The other prefers to demand what he wants despite everything and takes all he can. One speaks with the gravity of desire impossible to satisfy; he stays on the side of transcendence, taking refuge in the dignity of patience. In the other we have the relief of satisfied flesh, of appetite relished before all the world, and finally of the admission that superficiality is not such a bad thing after all. For Tatlıses, too, the city is woman; but both the forlorn, honourable male and the unfaithful, unattainable female have long since become history. Now the male wants his share of all the bounties of this world, 'cherry lips', 'rose-like breasts', and says so in public.[2] So, the absolute desire of old and the new era's appetite – this is the fundamental difference between Gencebay's 'I don't want your charity' and Tatlıses's 'Me Too'. And there is of course the difference of authenticity: Orhan Gencebay was a star at a time when popular culture in Turkey had not yet destroyed the halo of authenticity around the idols it created. But İbrahim Tatlıses realized that it was now futile to make an investment in authenticity. From the start he invented himself as his own imitation, his own parody. And that is why we always received 'Me Too' along with its parody, for example the line from another song on many people's lips in 1980s Turkey, 'You give it up to strangers, but not to Me?'[3]

Coming to relationships with fathers. In the 1970s Orhan Gencebay was the voice of conscience, something which could only be represented in Turkey by a male in those years: 'Big brother Orhan' defended the rights of the family against an unjust father. And that is what has changed: by the end of the 1980s the father had lost his former gravity and the family had cracked up. As for the stepbrother, he was not a member of the family anyway; the big city of the 1980s gave him the freedom, even if only for a moment, to be other than what he was, to be someone who could make his own voice heard instead of a phantom on his big brother's conscience. So if we are to speak of a new type of star rising in the 1990s in Turkey, he emerged not from the ranks of fathers or big brothers but of the stepbrothers of whose existence we had not even been aware. But if Gencebay was condemned to defeat by his insistence on resignation, excluded from the street whose voice he once embodied, Tatlıses was condemned from the start to be the spoiled child of the family who did not challenge the father with an eye to taking his place. On the faces of all the stars today who, like İbrahim Tatlıses, come from the countryside or rise from poverty, one can see the satisfaction of having finally made it, the lightweight feeling of representing no one but themselves, as much as the confidence of knowing that having once accomplished that, one way or another their desires will surely be met by the marketplace.

IV

For me there is still something lacking in this narrative. In Turkey we always tend to see that transformation in the cultural sphere, that explosion of wants which unbound the components of desire, as a manifestation of the 1980s. We think of the 1970s in terms like renunciation, patience and dignity. This perception is largely correct, but not entirely, for the cultural ambiance of the 1970s was not really so monolithic. It is forgotten that the first explosion of pornography in Turkey was in the 1970s. Between 1975 and 1980 there was a 'run on sex', to use the phrase current at that time; a great majority of the films made in Turkey during those five years were sex films.[4] True, it was a kind of pornography aimed at a small audience of male viewers who could go to the dark and dirty theatres where such films were shown. But that is precisely what made them the antithesis of the honourable 1970s. The ultimate moment of union found its unmediated expression in pornography, even if in comedic forms, to spite the voices always repeating the same story of unattainable women and luckless lovers. If the comical male figure who takes the woman instantly in films like *Şevket, Sacrifice to Lust*[5] is not the flip side of Gencebay's grave and pompous 'Lovers Are Never Happy', waving away the world with the back of his hand in the name of absolute desire, what is?

The explosion of desire which seemed to have begun in the 1980s was actually there in the 1970s, although squeezed into a very narrow space. Although the 1970s appear to have been years of renunciation when we look back on them today, they were in fact internally divided in a clear-cut way. On the one hand, there was a voice willing, with the energy provided by absolute desire, to oppose the law and call upon people to resist the seductions of the big city in expectation of a distant tomorrow: that was the voice that made Orhan Gencebay a star. On the other hand, there was a second voice unwilling and anyway unable to accept renunciation or to defy the law for the sake of the desired woman, a voice which from the very start adopted an obscene and comedic role circumscribed by infantile demands:

here the 'run on sex' came into play. But this second voice had a more important function than comic relief: the sublime, unattainable woman of absolute desire was replaced by a contemptible female divested of all transcendence, and sexuality as degradation supplanted desire as virtue. In trying to understand the modern world of the 1970s, we should not forget that these two displacements made up a single world, a single universe of desire, and that there desire was desire precisely because what was repressed on the one hand was provoked on the other. We had 'Let this World Sink', and we had *Şevket, Sacrifice to Lust*; both 'Console Me' and *Sex Till I Die*; both 'A Man Must Endure his Fate' and *Wild for Lust*. If there is a woman who arouses desire but leaves it unsatisfied, who shows what she has but does not give it up, there is also a woman who gives it up right then and there. If there is a big city which attracts but does not satisfy, there is a second big city provoking appetite and lust, ready to fulfil every desire. If there is an overblown discourse of love binding all desire to a grand narrative, there is also a copulation scene no narrative will accommodate.[6]

The message of Orhan Gencebay's discourse of resurrection, constructed out of generally religious but sometimes plainly leftist elements and delivered to the masses piling into the big city on the eve of Turkey's new life as a consumer society, should be analysed within this polarity. The polarization of content is immediately evident when we glance at newspapers from the 1970s. On the one hand, articles on hunger strikes, resistance and boycott; on the other, advertisements for night clubs and music-halls which, in *Hürriyet*, for example, regularly took up four or five pages. On the one hand, custodial arrests by the police, clashes between workers and police, strikes and political meetings; on the other, advertisements for alluring singers, striptease shows, sex shows, and free 'sex records'. On the one hand, Gencebay's bodiless, face-less cruel women; on the other, the invariable female with a steady gaze, false eyelashes, slightly moist lips, puffy curled hair and an artificial flower pinned behind her ear. One of them addressed the reader as if to say, 'Repress your desire that you may organize', while the other said, 'Abandon yourself to infantile desire.'

The 1980 military coup put an end to this 'run on sex' in Turkey, along with many other things. For a short while: a second 'run on sex', which in a sense aimed to pornographicize the entire culture, ensued immediately afterwards, in the second half of the 1980s. But it was different in several respects. First of all, it was far more widespread; not only meant for men in the dark and dirty halls of inferior movie theatres, it was offered to everyone, man, woman and child. Second, it acquired a far more 'cultured' tone, thanks to the language constructed by the media, advertising and entertainment sectors. This was not a subculture that defined itself by prohibition, secrecy and shame, or by a goofiness expected to bring relief from such things; it was offered as culture itself. Perhaps most important of all, there was behind it a promise of freedom.[7] When the brakes were taken off the desire confined during the 1970s to a homely, comedic 'run on sex', it was liberated from its degradation and succeeded in offering itself to the entire society as a proposition of modern culture.[8]

V

More distant history may shed clearer light for analysing the recent. In *Civilization and its Discontents* Freud returned once more to the relationship between culture and the pleasure and reality principles. He wrote of how the pleasure principle in man is gradually transformed under the influence of the external world into the more humble reality principle. According to Freud, this was the source of discontent in civilization today; people have been forced by external reality to whittle down their desires for happiness and freedom. But he also said that the instruments we employ to defend ourselves from threats issuing from the sources of suffering belong to civilization as well. Culture is founded upon renunciation, upon cultural frustration; but man subdues desire to his own use only by renouncing it, and 'by damping down the fire of his own sexual excitation' tames the natural force of fire: 'This great cultural conquest was thus the reward for his renunciation of instinct.'[9]

There Freud moved on to speak of two requisites of civilization: justice and freedom. According to Freud, individual freedom is not something brought about by civilization; on the contrary, it is something civilization restricts. The first requisite of civilization is justice, usually at the price of individual freedom. In other words, justice is the assurance that a law once made will not be broken in favour of an individual, and thus puts restrictions upon individual freedom. Civilization has traded a portion of security for a portion of man's potential for happiness, overcoming the dangerous aggression of the individual by ensuring its control through the internal authority of the superego. But the discontent which ensues from this repression leads to the second requisite, the wish for freedom.

In this essay I have tried to view Turkey's recent history through the different dynamics of desire and culture. It has not been my intention to claim that one is more in the right, or more authentic, than the other. By linking the two dynamics with the demands of justice and freedom, I am not saying that those demands will always express themselves as the absolute polarities we in Turkey experienced for the space of twenty years. But it should not be forgotten that they are always in tension by virtue of the nature of culture itself. In Turkey's recent past, within what can be considered a short space of time, there has been a transition from a justice-centred sum of demands to one having freedom at the centre. The 1970s' demand for justice gave way to the 1980s' demand for freedom because it was not all that just, because it put restrictions upon individual freedoms, whittled down the people's demand for happiness and, perhaps most importantly of all, because it fell victim to power. But in these days when the demand for freedom is not all that free, when it leads to new forms of captivity as the mere freedom to consume and, perhaps most importantly of all, remains indifferent to threats issuing from the sources of suffering; in these days when the gap between those with opportunity and those without grows wider, when crimes and unjust wars carried out by the hand of the state make accomplices of us all, do we not have need again of a demand for justice?

Surely there will be tension between those who wish this world would sink and those who cry 'Me too!' But, rather than present each of these demands as the ideological preference of a different generation, it would be better to see culture's differing forms of discontent therein, and discern how they are directed and transformed into a social imperative.

SIX

Death of the Stranger

I

IN THE EARLY 1980s the entire front page of one of Turkey's major newspapers was taken up by a photograph of the porno film star Feri Cansel. The photograph had been taken in the municipal morgue. The caption read: 'Feri Cansel shot dead by her lover'.

It was doubtless the photograph itself which caused this piece of news, something that would normally be reported on a paper's third page or at best the bottom half of the first, to migrate to the place of pride. For those living in 1970s' Turkey the name of Feri Cansel was synonymous with nudity, and here she was naked but now lying lifeless in a morgue drawer. The photographer had obviously found in the morgue an opportunity to do his work just as he liked; one could count the bullet holes in Cansel's lifeless body.

The 1980s were years when newspapers kept out of politics; executions, the disappearance of prisoners in police custody and deaths under torture were reported in barely visible notices buried in the back pages. Those who remember the period will recall that the front page was devoted almost entirely to family tragedies, crimes of passion and madness – if we don't count the reports of 'anarchy and terror' intended to legitimize the coup. Husbands murdering wives, mothers murdering children, brothers murdering brothers. And, of course, traffic accidents. It was in those years that I first saw horrific images of road accidents, bodies left twisted in the ruins of cars, lifeless eyes frozen in terror, corpses ripped to shreds, burned to a crisp, one after another and all arranged as if part of a single picture. In those years there was a sudden, highly visible explosion in scenes of death.

Censorship was one of the reasons for the explosion. When politics were removed from the agenda after the coup and the state violence that became an ordinary fact of daily life then could not be spoken of, the papers moved on to less dangerous arenas to find news to shock their readers. They kept busy with the non-political faces of violence, treating violence as if it were a feature of private life alone. In fact in Turkey as in many other countries, the press always keeps such stories handy to use at a pinch. But during the years I am speaking of newspapers pressed to find a lead story would use up these spare stories every day as the primary source for huge headlines in the blackest of black fonts.

But there was also a death not allowed on the agenda, a death which could not be spoken of in public. Execution, torture, civil war. It was as if because that death could not be spoken, because the rage felt against the state could not be uttered and public avenues of mourning were cut off, death returned in other forms, even if by roundabout routes, to demand its share. In fact it was not only people or those dear to them who died but beloved thoughts, ideals and relationships. It was in those years that scenes of mayhem, murder and suicide first left their stamp on the press agenda in such an obvious way. Or it was then that I noticed it, with all those headlines screaming 'Atrocity!' and the constant fixation with corpses to which we were all reduced, our way of looking at death was palpably transformed. Now the public language for speaking of death became a pornographic diction which treated it as a wholly external trauma, an alien, and exciting, scourge. The nakedness of Feri Cansel, who had been the object of a pornographic gaze all her life, captured now not on film but in a morgue drawer, seemed so striking to me because it was one of the first examples of this transformation to which we are all now inured. And because it constituted a genuinely heart-rending irony: As if the 1970s' porn star had fallen prey to the media this time because she made an issue of repressed death rather than repressed sexuality, representing, in all its nakedness, the death which had been pushed beyond the borders of our lives. Perhaps the pornography of death was not yet ready to replace the pornography of sex, but it settled right down beside it.

In the more than twenty years since, we have learned to be inured to other representations of death as well. Guerrillas with their clothes pulled up to expose their half-naked bodies like forbidden documents, militants riddled with bullets from policemen's guns, soldiers now mere coffins decorated with the crescent moon and star of the Turkish flag, women stabbed full of holes by their lovers, children strangled by mothers gone mad

– what does all this death we now receive as a continuous image of horror displayed in newspapers and television bulletins every day say to us about death? What are the feelings aroused in us by the scenes of savagery from distant lands where 'death runs rampant', confronting us every few days on the front page of the high-circulation newspapers *Hürriyet* or *Sabah*? What does the severed head of a Somalian explain to us when we do not know where or how the man lived, who killed him or why? What does it mean for beheadings by axe in Saudi Arabia or hangings by crane in Iran to be shown on television screens over and over again? How does it affect us to see Palestinian youths hold up the body parts of friends blown to bits by Israeli bombs? These quotations from life stories ending in violent death – whether they take place in countries always seemingly far off no matter how near they may be, or in Turkey's own forsaken hamlets and seemingly distant shanty towns ringing the cities – form a modern language offering all to the marketplace as a single, giant image of 'Horror!' How does that language affect our view of a world death has constructed through images of torn-up bodies?

II

In his *Western Attitudes toward Death*, the French historian Philippe Ariès wrote of how Western civilization's view of death did not change much from the Middle Ages to the mid-nineteenth century. For nearly one thousand years, death was a familiar thing; the realization of a fate which did not annihilate personality but put it to sleep. Death was experienced as a communal cult, a ceremony in which the person on his deathbed was a participant. People were no more strangers to the death of loved ones than they were to their own. They died at home; all their loved ones, including children, were allowed in the room.[1]

Western Attitudes toward Death is the story of how this familiarity changed. Towards the end of the eighteenth century an interesting development occurred in the cities. As the deaths of others, rather than one's own, grew in importance, the language of death acquired a romantic character; a dying person's words and behaviour took on a significance never accorded them before. Death was now encircled by an eloquent decor; it became a personal cult characterized by an unprecedented degree of ostentation. This mode has continued to our day, and according to Ariès drew more from positivism than religion. As it developed hand in hand with patriotism and nationalism, the cult of death involved the exaltation of death as an object of emotion. By the nineteenth century death was something seen everywhere; the space accorded to cemeteries had expanded; funeral ceremonies, visits to graves, mourning costumes and graves themselves had taken on an ostentatious character.

Ariès tells us that the extreme visibility of death concealed an atrophy of feeling. In fact by the time this impressive decor was demolished, death had become unnameable. It was no longer the familiar end one met with resignation or, as in the Romantic era, a dramatic sign; it had been transformed into something too horrific to name and, moreover, shameful. That was one reason why the deathbed was moved to the hospital, for the good of the dying person's loved ones and the good of society. The discomfort brought about by the macabre presence of death in the midst of happy life, the distress which mortality caused those left alive, the emotional upheaval the deathbed scene created in those who would go on with their lives – all necessitated the interdiction against death, which first appeared in the United States at the beginning of the twentieth century and spread from there to industrialized Europe.

Like many European scholars working in the second half of the twentieth century, Ariès addressed what modern civilization, formerly identified with liberation, repressed; the prohibition it internalized. But reading Ariès now my mind is preoccupied with two questions at once. First, to what extent does Turkey share in this narrative? Which of its elements are part of the story here? Second, where does the quality of spectacle that the ubiquity death has acquired in today's modern culture, be it in Turkey or elsewhere, fit into this story? Can one speak of an interdiction against death in a world where newspapers and television shows, in order to shock people gradually become inured to the scenes of death which first transfixed them, increase a little more each day the dose of violence in the images they present, seeking out ever more 'live' images of death to compete for an audience share? Can one say that death is repressed in an environment where several times a year, under the heading of 'a special news report', we are exposed to executions carried out in an Asian or African country? Can one speak of denial in a cultural milieu which not only makes a provocative display of death but bombards us with horrifically dark, uncanny contents once banished to subterranean realms? Is this a return of the repressed? If so, how does the return occur?

First, it is important to emphasize Turkey's difference in this respect. Here most of the images of death to which we are subject convey a political message. A politics of intimidation, an atmosphere of threat: a cautionary tale of the danger in defying the state, a message letting you know what will happen to you 'if you stray from the path'. How else can one explain the almost instant transmission everywhere of images taken by state cameras of the smoking bodies of inmates burned alive in the 'Return to Life' operation?[2] In Turkey every child grows up seeing in newspapers and on television the corpse of that same accursed creature under various names – the bandit, the stick-up man, the anarchist, the terrorist – frightened at first but soon learning to be inured. Every child internalizes at an early age a political message constructed not as a believable ideology but more often as an out-and-out lie, a state politics that identifies the word 'compassion'[3] with outright cruelty; and every child grows into adulthood learning that, unless willing to fight that cruelty with the same cruelty, he or she must not get mixed up in anything at all. In a land of political murder perpetrated by agents unknown, images of death are always accompanied by a political fear.

That political content with its ever-present weight has gradually become articulated to a more modern tale. Ariès wrote that modern society's interdiction against death was transformed within religious discourse into an expression of the meaningless of the world and within the family into an unacceptable separation. In modern society 'my' death became 'your' death, the death of the beloved other. However much we do not want to name that death, it steals away the entire meaning of life. To the extent that Turkey has modernized, it also shares in that denial. But it is precisely here that we must speak of a realm into which Ariès does not venture, of something which has become evident during the quarter century since *Western Attitudes toward*

Death was published: the return, in one way or another, of repressed death. For in the modern culture of today, the 'you' of 'your death', the other, is no longer a person we love. In the extreme representations we see each day, death seems the death of someone who really is 'other', someone who touches our lives not at all, someone who is always morally, socially and politically distant from us – the death of a stranger. Not a stranger whose death takes away with it the meaning of this world, not the death of an other leaving us with incurable wounds, but, on the contrary, a stranger's death reinforcing our egos and strengthening our moral and political reflexes. Whenever we look at the corpses on television screens or in the pages of newspapers, it is him we see: he is a pervert, a terrorist, a murderer, a monster; victim of a sudden loss of sanity, a natural or social disaster, an accident, or violence turned against the self. From morning till night we are faced with representations of death; but in none of them is death the inevitable end met by all. No image contains death as a natural process, as a preordained end, as mortality. On the contrary, death is represented in all of them as an extraordinary event, an exorbitant excess, a perversion, a catastrophe, a travesty. Perhaps no television show moderator in Turkey has ever made a scandal of his death by shooting himself in the head before millions of viewers, but if, for example, the dying summon to their side television announcers instead of loved ones, or if people are able to call in on television shows and speak about lost loved ones in a weirdly calm tone, or on the contrary as if talking about something illegal or scandalous, is the chief reason not only that social channels of mourning are cut off, but that the form of discourse for speaking of the death of a distant stranger is now the only one left for speaking of a loved one's death?

Scandal works to serve two different purposes. First, it presents death as the act of a monstrous spirit, a perversion, a disaster whose perpetrator remains unknown; scandal cleanses death of its social and political content; it conflates all unnatural deaths – traffic accident and execution, death by torture and traffic accident, political bloodbath and personal loss of sanity, death by hunger strike and suicide, civil war and murder – along a single axis of horror. Second, while scandal confronts us with images of extraordinary death every day, it thrusts death itself beyond the course of ordinary life. For us death is an aberration, not the natural end which comes to all. Death is pushed out, certainly out of the house; it occurs at dangerous intersections, on slippery roads, dark and dirty streets, in desolate hamlets, in prison cells, in extreme states of mind. It is banished to shanty towns on the edges of cities, to rural areas or far-off countries where completely different rules obtain, to Africa, Arabia, Afghanistan. For us death is the fate suffered in those countries, the rule in far-off places. Even when it returns to civilization, to the place from which it was banished, it is always seen as sign of that rural darkness, as an irrational content seeping in from there; for us death is extraordinary, shocking, traumatic, while for them it is sign of an everyday horror. Just as Turkey is viewed in the West as a land of death, a distant hinterland where dread reigns, so Turkey views Somalia, Afghanistan and, more importantly, its own East: as a region where death roams free, where insanity is the rule.

Behind the persistent banishment of death to distant lands there is in fact the wish to expel it from time. In a world where the sense of time, transiency and mortality is unimportant, everyone is always a child and so should remain. That is why we watch the scenes of death passing before our eyes as if the exploding bombs, the collapsing homes, the bullet-riddled, twisted, flattened figures were cartoons. As we receive the death of the stranger, we vacillate between fascination and indifference, the monotony of our lives interrupted by the guilty pleasure of knowing it can take nothing away from us. We watch death as scandal pleased to be ordinary people with ordinary lives; our lives are not that extreme, and we are not abnormal like that. I speak not only of situations where death acquires a political content. To see a young man addicted to sniffing glue slash his throat with a knife and leap into the void from the roof of an apartment building does not make us more sensitive to such sufferings. On the contrary, it strengthens our sense that the home is the best refuge from the danger stalking the cities, that our lives are the safest possible lives. But there is the other side of that process: those savage images both thrust the death no one can escape out of our lives as an extraordinary horror, and transform the social violence we can escape into an event so routine we can afford to be indifferent to it.

I said that Ariès does not venture into that new face of the interdiction against death. But clues to how the repressed has returned on another level are not lacking in his book. He speaks of the contempt for authority which the interdiction against death brought along with it, of how eroticism was intertwined with death throughout the period stretching from the sixteenth to the eighteenth century, and how in several literary works of the eighteenth century, those of the Marquis de Sade above all, death began to be viewed as a transgression which, like sexual intercourse, cuts a person off from everyday life, from rational society, from the monotony of ordinary experience, and conveys him to the realm of the irrational; shed of its familiarity, death has now formed an alliance with eroticism in the realm of imagination. The more than quarter century that has passed since *Western Attitudes toward Death* was published forces us to think in greater detail about the nature of this alliance. For there is an aspect to the attitude towards death which cannot be explained in terms of interdiction/defiance or law/transgression dichotomies. This is particularly so in the world of today where defiance is practised less by art and literature than by the media of mass communication.

III

Twenty years before Ariès's book was published, the British anthropologist Geoffrey Gorer wrote an article titled 'Pornography of Death', and ten years later published his book *Death, Grief and Mourning*.[4] His book contains the results of interviews conducted in England with persons from different social classes for the purpose of demonstrating how people's attitudes towards death had changed. In this study, which appears in Ariès's bibliography and serves as the inspiration for his chapter 'Forbidden Death', Gorer wrote that in the twentieth century mourning was denied to both society and the individual. For an ethics of enjoyment founded upon the taking of pleasure no matter what, mourning is a transgression of the imperative to do nothing that might diminish the enjoyment of others – a transgression of the right to happiness as a duty. A society which views death as a source of shame and disgust will see mourning not as a psychological necessity but as a weakness, and moreover a disease. Thus the mourner is treated tolerantly, but as a person who is ill.

Perhaps even more important among Gorer's conclusions is that death and sexuality exchanged places in the twentieth century. As death was banished from our lives, sexuality filled the space left empty; and now instead of sexuality, death was taboo. Just as sexual intercourse and birth had in the previous two centuries been received with feelings of guilt as shameful, disgusting things which should be kept hidden, so was death in the twentieth. Now it was death which bore the charge of a guilty pleasure, not sex. That was what led Gorer to speak of a 'pornography of death'. The images of beheadings carried out in Saudi Arabia and broadcast constantly on Turkish television screens come to mind here. The executioner lowers his axe, and we see it; we watch the film recording of this over and over again; but right at the moment when the victim's head is about to be severed from his body, there falls across the screen a shadow reminiscent of the blackout bands which used to cover the sex organs of women in nude images. Here death really has taken the place of sex.

'Pornography' is the correct term for the dichotomy in our approach to death today because it signifies interdiction and transgression at one and the same time. When we speak of a 'pornography of death', we speak of a death which takes its metaphor from sexuality; but here sexuality should be thought of not merely as something repressed but as a Foucauldian region of secreted pleasure forced into speech. Only then can we understand why society today reproduces images of death without cease, breaking on another plane the silence felt before death, and drives people to represent death as scandal. So, here there are at once two apparently contradictory modes that in fact complement each other somehow. Two faces of modern experience: if on the one hand there is the rejection of mourning in the name of happiness, duty or health, the incapacity to tolerate even illness let alone death in those close to us, the inability to somehow find words to speak with children about death, on the other there is the desire to watch, almost spellbound – as we once were by sexuality, eyes averted slightly, slightly disgusted, yet with intense curiosity, enormous pleasure – extraordinary death, savage crime, inconceivable madness which allows none to be moved by sorrow, permits not the tiniest crumb of mourning.

It is this double mode which has left its stamp on the new cultural environment in Turkey. The society of spectacle began its work by creating shiny objects; dazzling, gleaming objects which spread light on everything around them. There was a moment at the start when death, horror and dread were repressed, when everything was gilded, and to the degree that an object offered to the marketplace succeeded at that, it was attractive, seductive and consumable. But today the world of spectacle brings with it things not shiny at all. Everything can be painted with gilt – the darkest contents of the undermost levels of consciousness, repressed energies, destructive impulses, the freakish, hideous and repulsive. Yes, the repressed returns today, but not as it was when first repressed; it returns transformed into something else. That is why it is not possible to explain people's attitudes towards death today merely in terms of 'interdiction' or 'repression'. But perhaps most importantly of all, the role forced upon the weak in this weird alliance between interdiction and arousal was obvious from the start. Why are horrific images of death always taken from poor countries far away? Why are third-page reports of murder always about people treated as minorities, if not in number then in culture, about a poverty seen in itself as the source of weakness and irrationality, of disgust or shame? Death must be far from us: it was here that Bataille sought the reason for fear of poor people. 'The rich fear workers, and the petit bourgeois panic at the thought they may become workers, because in their eyes the poor are closer to death', Bataille wrote in *Literature and Evil*: 'We are even at times more disgusted by the filth, the impotence, the squalor of dark and dirty streets which bring on death than we are by death itself.'[5]

They disgust us, and therefore give great pleasure. Turkey continues to make a myth of the death of soldiers and a cult of the death of famous personalities. Death is a stranger in all of them, in all of them there is denial. But it is no coincidence that the real stuff of today's pornographic death is not the cult of corpses, not magnificent funerals and monumental tombs, but unclaimed cadavers exposed to public view. It is here one must seek the real difference between the funeral of a famous pop star attracting a gathering of thousands and the torn-up corpse of a third-page hero; between the dignified burial of a famous businessman and Feri Cansel's naked body stuffed into a morgue drawer.

SEVEN

Child of Agony

ON THE wooden carts of itinerant postcard-sellers parked in
many Istanbul neighbourhoods – in Şişli, Beşiktaş, Aksaray
– pictures of sad children may be found among the portraits of
nudes, brave soldiers and pastoral scenes. Postcards featuring
the beautiful faces of suffering children with tears welling up in
the springs of their sad eyes. One of them was particularly well
known in Turkey some twenty-five years ago. The picture of a
small boy with helplessly pouted lips and tears pouring down
his round cheeks. Posters were produced later as well, hung in
grocer's shops, coffee houses and workplaces next to portraits
of Atatürk and Kenan Evren, leader of the 1980 coup and later
president. It was the long-distance bus drivers working routes
between rural areas and big cities who loved that picture most.
The weeping child stared at us for a long time from the huge
posters hung in the back windows of inter-city buses in those
years. He was not much like the usual representation of agony in

Turkey then: mistreated, undersized, uncared-for village children who symbolized neglect. He had neatly combed blonde hair, huge blue eyes, clean clothes and a bright, clean face. He seemed to be from a good family and to have fallen on hard times rather than been born into suffering. He made you think less of poverty suffered from birth, less of a lack that had always been there, than of a blow suffered later, and most of all of a motherless or orphaned child. He seemed to sulk at the world because of a misfortune he could not understand. In a piece written about that picture in those years, Murat Belge attributed its popularity to the guilt Turkish society bore towards children. He wrote that this boy with the beautiful eyes, who belonged to no one but could be anyone's child, awakened feelings of guilt slumbering for years in the depths of people's consciences.[1]

I thought it was less a matter of guilt than the feeling of being unjustly treated that when adults looked at that picture they identified with the agonized child. They felt like abused children themselves, they saw their own suffering in his face and pitied themselves in the person of that child. This identification plays a part in all images of war, disaster or suffering which focus on the sad face of a child. In all of them the face of the child enters circulation as the most concise expression of the pain adults feel. But there is always an excess of meaning there as well. In fact the picture does not tell of suffering but of suffering one does not deserve. The child there is symbol of the blameless victim, punished though innocent, sacrificed upon the altar of unjust laws. Moreover, the child of agony also represents a certain resistance to his viewers. He signifies honour preserved despite all, more than an irreparable terrorization experienced at a young age, an utter helplessness or dreadful rage that will out sooner or later. He is profoundly wounded, badly bruised at a tender age; but in spite of that, in fact because of it, he has not given up his struggle against a cruel world, he is still on his feet. It is as if everything were suddenly reversed: the agony of a child in a vulgar world now stands before us as the source of honour, virtue and goodness of heart.

As for his being blonde. At least in this case, Turkey seemed to have found its sad boy hero not among its own stunted children – who remind it of the reasons for its own childishness, its poverty, its Eastern roots – but in this Western child suffering for reasons unknown to us. Like the faces of the smiling blonde children who appear in most children's books published in Turkey, like the fat, blue-eyed infants in television commercials for baby food or diapers and the well-washed street children of Yeşilçam,[2] this face has despite all its orphaned pathos been purified of any psychic stain, any resentment or violence born of childhood suffering. And precisely for that reason, to the extent it is pure of all the negative feeling that goes with suffering, to the extent it displays endurance in sorrow, honour in trial, this face became a metaphor of pain.

Child of Agony

The tearful child's poster is not the first or last of agonized child images to be popular in Turkey. We also find them in the first examples of popular modern Turkish city literature. In almost all of his novels, Kemalettin Tuğcu[3] described well-brought-up male children lost and friendless in big cities, pathetic apprentices to coffee-sellers and ironmongers, ill-starred porter and newspaper boys. Almost all these children suffer due to some fateful calamity which befalls them after better days. Almost all are orphaned in one way or another; either their fathers are dead or have fallen into decline, gone bankrupt or been put in prison. Mothers are always helpless, younger siblings always sick. Tuğcu's novels always follow the same formula, with the story of a male child in the pitiless city who takes responsibility for the family at a tender age, brings the scattered family back together, finds himself a father figure or master in trade, or learns a trade on his own. Tuğcu exalted two things: childhood and endurance in suffering. In this setting, where endurance in suffering is set before us as an almost national ideal, and identified with childhood absolutely, the child in agony is the true embodiment of all national virtues. We are continually presented with children who are ill-treated but honourable, bruised but conscientious, oppressed but steadfast, sad but good-hearted. And so all of these novels end with the victory of a quick-witted, sensitive, good-natured little pauper who summons adults to the right path, softens the icy hearts of old men, and reforms good-for-nothing rich kids. This big-little child speaks well and makes grand, profound statements, opening to us the doors to a world where adults need consoling and children are up to the task. And there is something else he does: he brings the good news that subjection to poverty in early youth, trials suffered at a tender age, evil faced down at the beginning of life, all can have an ameliorating effect; virtue is born of agony, honour of poverty, and good of evil. That is what never changes in these novels. However bad things are, the child of agony will overcome poverty through struggle and become a noble, self-respecting, model human being.

That must be why both adults and children loved the Ayşecik films made in the 1960s and early 1970s – the first one an adaptation of a Tuğcu novel – and the Ömercik, Sezercik and Yumurcak films that followed them. In most of those films a fatherless child, forced to suffer a fate he does not deserve, struggles all alone to stay alive in the big bad city. But the films were the product of an era when the big city had not yet come to mean a place where the weak are utterly helpless. And so these films, like Tuğcu's novels, end with the victory of the child, despite all the tears he cried. The big-little baby girl angel Ayşecik, or the little lion Sezercik, using his wits, face down all cruel odds with the help of their poor neighbours; they liberate their fathers from prison, their mothers from the hospital, and hold their families together; and if not, they at least go on to find happy, often wealthy, homes for themselves. That is the invariable formula of all Yeşilcam films in which parents need saving and children are saviours. As viewers we identified with the child hero who struggles against wrong, who establishes justice, takes up the role of guardian of the family at a tender age; but in fact we were weeping at how we had never been able to grow up ourselves, while finding in that a strength never afforded in reality to adults. We are children; but it is our job to save adults from evil, defend justice against wrong, and resist this brutal world. Despite the fact that we are children; in fact precisely because we are. All these films representing children as wise and resilient are in fact expressions of an adult struggle to find something loveable in a luckless fate, in a powerlessness as social as it is familial; in short in the misfortune of never having been able to grow up.

In fact all these themes are found in fairy tales as well, and the image of the 'saviour child' acquired a new halo in Romantic literature. In the so insistent repetition of this image in the popular urban culture, in the determination to see a local virtue in immaturity, there is a part played by Turkish society's struggle to overcome its own childishness in the face of the modern West, to transform a ridiculous, stunted destiny and reverse the image of a 'childish society' reflected in the mirror held up by the West. These films set the stage for feelings of inadequacy to be identified with innocence, and innocence with heroism. Upon that stage the child of agony symbolizes a belittled local virtue, a potential for purification from all degeneracy – represented by the spoiled rich, by dance halls and dens of sin, by the corrupting influence of money. In the story of the child who emerges from his trials victorious in the end, adults could engender a national, local, Eastern pride out of the insurmountable poverty to which they'd been subjected. It is a kind of urban legend: to have been forced to grow up too young – in other words, to be robbed of childhood – and therefore forced to remain children forever, will bring us power as well as pain.

III

The poster of the weeping child was the harbinger of a new phase in Turkish society's struggle to find something loveable in luckless fate; it was one of the first examples of the 'agony explosion' of the 1980s. The 'child of agony' concept took its name from the title of a song by Little Emrah, a child singer who became famous in the mid-1980s, and the film of the same name in which he starred. Another Little Emrah film of those years, *The Humbled*, seems to have reinforced the agonized child image. The 1980s were a time when Turkish society, confronted by an unjust political regime after a military coup, found itself once more in the position of a child and forced to find something loveable in that luckless fate. Not only images of weeping children and agonized songs screamed by child singers, but the whole setting in which the big city was once more identified with pain, and pain with childhood, was much loved in those years. I speak not only of Little Emrah, nor of the other child singers whose melancholy was rapidly transformed into brash vulgarity as their numbers and earnings increased; not only of an industry, but of a society ready to have its suffering embodied in that cliché, which found once more in the child of agony the traces of its own powerlessness and tried once more to make of that powerlessness a national virtue. And let us not separate ourselves from that society so neatly. Was not there something similar in our fascination during those years with Oğuz Atay's clumsy, childish heroes unschooled in life and Ece Ayhan's 'dead middle-school drop-outs', his 'pale pauper's rebellion'.[4]

The weeping child in the poster was perhaps the last sad blonde child hero of a society which had long gazed lovingly on the suffering faces of well-washed children from good families – those Occidental victims of the city without mercy – the Ayşeciks and Ömerciks and Sezerciks of the silver screen. From

Tuğcu's friendless apprentices to Yeşilçam's orphans, from the sad postcard children to the 'child of agony' image of the 1980s, there had in fact been little change in the outlines of the mould. But in the mid-1980s, when Turkey discovered its own Eastern face, its own rural populations, its Kurds pouring into the cities – and discovered also that their fate was something which could be bought and sold – a new content began to seep into the mould. The sad child acquired a darker, swarthier, and more masculine countenance. The blonde gaiety of Ömercik was no longer convincing, and it was left behind. What did not change, however, was that the 'child of agony' story was always set up working backwards from the moment when the mistreated child emerged victorious. What was presented to us as the child of agony was in fact the face of that long-suffering, stunted boy photographed at the moment of success in the big city, when he got rich, even if he never found a family; when he managed to cheat his Oriental destiny. And partly because of that, despite all the negative content that might go along with suffering, this sad face could remain an image of virtue, innocence and honour, just as it had been in the novels of Tuğcu and the films of Yeşilçam. The pitiful child was left fatherless, homeless and directionless in the pitiless city, but precisely because of that he was both injured and innocent, vulnerable and resistant, both a child and a man.

We mustn't forget that the image gradually acquired a political emphasis, drawing its real power from the ongoing war in the East, in the regions of Turkey where the Kurds live. What orphaned the child was less the loss of a real father than the lack of a just one. And what made that privation believable was the image of a father willing to sacrifice his children for no good reason, the image of innocent children punished; the image of a state willing to sacrifice its people for no good reason, the image of innocent people punished. Although the 'woman of agony' who emerged around that time was as short-lived as the singer Bergen who named her (Bergen was murdered by her husband),[5] the agonized boy had a long life in Turkish culture. Songs were sung about him, poems written, movies made. For a long time traces of his image could be read on the faces of almost all male stars with rural origins, not only child singers. The spoiled city girl who finds happiness and a chance for redemption in the ill-treated boy who gives her back her long-lost innocence was an oft-repeated theme of 1990s' films.[6]

IV

What really interests me here is less the history of the image than the moment when it became a lie. Ten years after the 'child of agony' explosion in the 1980s, the image was suddenly no longer an essential thread in the cultural fabric. It became one of hundreds of different images in the marketplace. It lost its former popularity and, more importantly, its former credibility. But the peculiar thing was that the change occurred just when suffering became most visible in the faces of children, when the streets of big cities filled with children who really had been treated unjustly, as Kurdish villages were emptied and real orphans appeared in the big cities. Oddly, the image lost its credibility when it was confronted by what it represented, and in fact because it had been. Moreover, as newspaper and television reports of 'child violence' increased, the image of a child's face lost its power to symbolize suffering. The image of the vulnerable child who brings justice although himself wronged at a tender age, gave way to that of the child lying in wait in the city, ready to commit crimes at any moment. The child who had for long years been at the centre of a much-loved romance of the victim, symbolizing a national feeling of orphanhood and an Oriental pride, now leapt out suddenly before us as an object of fear, a figure of dread.

What is peculiar about this story is that the problem of homeless children living on the streets had in fact become an issue during the years when the child of agony image became popular. But it was obvious from the start that street children would not be able to represent a suffering the whole society shared; they could not symbolize a national feeling of privation. However sorry people may have felt for street children at first, they were a problem not because they were suffering but because they committed crimes; not because they were victims of the cruel city but, on the contrary, because they threatened it, in short because they were, as early magazine news coverage put it, 'child criminals'. In other words, for the middle class these children were from the start lacking in the innocence which defined the 'child of agony', lacking in the honour that came of surviving in the big city without a father, the virtue which derived its strength from endurance in the face of suffering. Somehow their luckless fate always led to a life of crime, not to a honourable manhood like that of Yumurcak or Little Emrah or Tuğcu's children sleeping under bridges. They were always mentioned in connection with evil things, as suspects in the horrors sensationalized on page three. Doğuş, the street child who rose to stardom as a singer, was no exception.[7] When he sang his sad songs with a tear in his eye, even news announcers clasped to their breasts this youth who transformed suffering into success. But it didn't take long for his bad record, his thefts and other crimes to come out; his story was over the moment it began. A childhood spent on the streets just never could be promoted from a source of class fear to a national image of suffering.

This lack of overlap between image and reality shows us two things at once. First, the 'child of agony' was a lie. For it could only be an image of innocence by concealing the true causes of oppression, and the horror and pent-up rage that goes along with it – that was how it made suffering into something loveable.[8] Second, it was the end of an era in Turkey; suffering would no longer be represented by orphan children, by steadfast apprentices who succeeded in becoming model human beings in the end, by impoverished children who found their way all alone in the big city. For no matter how false those images were, they derived their credibility from a time when the rural populations of Turkey had not yet emptied into the city with all their violence and poverty, a time when the middle class had not yet perceived poverty as a threat coming from the masses. Today the story of the pauper child who wins out by using his wits, without recourse to violence, with the help of good-hearted masters in trade or the support of his poor neighbourhood, has lost its credibility not only for a middle class which has long since abandoned the ideal of frugality but for the poor themselves as well. These are days when misery is regarded not as an object of sympathy but of fear; when poverty is not the face of a cruel fate but mere personal ineptitude. The stuff of popular imagination today is not stories of suffering children but the 'reality shows' which have invaded television news programming and the page-three sensationalism constructed by the major newspaper conglomerates. They tell us stories of the suffering poor as a dangerous mob in which oppression begets rage and pain begets crime.

V

Yet we should pause to consider how our mentality underwent such an important transformation in just a few decades. How is it that we now regard as an object of fear the child we identified with innocence, vulnerability and virtue for so many years? What older fears are combined in the class fear which street children inspire? What does it mean for a child to symbolize the uncanny?

Philippe Ariès's analysis in his *Centuries of Childhood* of how we got from a Middle Ages that had no image of childhood as something clearly demarcated from adulthood to a modern world in which childhood is a stable concept provides clues which may help us to answer these questions. The child who had long been seen as a 'miniature adult', sharing with adults the same spaces, the same clothes and the same games, began to be differentiated in eighteenth-century European societies as the locus of a different knowledge and centre of a different sort of attraction. Thus life acquired two separate spheres, one the world of adults and another outside of it for children. According to Ariès, two notions accompanied the modern discovery of childhood. First, the notion that children are basically good and innocent, not inclined to sin or evil, and for that reason should be protected from the world of adults. Second, children are weak and ignorant, and so must be disciplined and educated. If an adult is someone in control of her emotions, discreet and prudent, observant and watchful, a child is someone who should be constantly watched because she can at any moment go too far and lose control. While Ariès analysed Western European societies, and in particular their middle classes, he provided clues shedding light on the basic characteristics of attitudes towards children in the modern era elsewhere as well.[9] In this new understanding of childhood – and in the gaze turned in fact towards not only childhood but also the savage, the primitive and the East conceived of as a kind of childhood – there was a hidden dichotomy which spawned two different attitudes. In so far as the child was innocent, uncorrupted and pure, she was an object of nostalgia; but in so far as she needed to be disciplined from birth and trapped in a web of knowledge, her nature was basically savage, wild and dangerous.

One source of our fear of children is that second, usually suppressed, aspect. Within that fear is concealed the insight that the unrestrained child, like the unrestrained mob, is an agent of savagery. And that is why we today can regard as uncanny the child whom until recent times we thought of as an innocent being. For despite all the tales of innocence we have told about children, in modern society the child is from the start a recondite metaphor of the mob. Just as we regard the mob, with its incapacity for self-control and irrational nature which must be reined in, as a child in need of discipline, so do we regard the child, with its dangerous nature that must be suppressed, as the mob. There is a Janus-faced metaphor here. Just as the unrestrained mob, like the unrestrained child, is rebellious, savage and uncanny, so is the unrestrained child rebellious, savage and uncanny like the unrestrained mob.

Child of Agony

I am thinking of how we perceive the street children whose numbers are increasing in the big cities of Turkey with every passing day. They are individuals who share a common fate, yet for someone passing them on the street they are not single, separate persons but an army of children on the move, a herd on stampede. A dark crowd which emerges into the light of day from the wild hurly-burly of the city's dark and dirty corners only to return there again, a rabble able to scatter in all directions at any moment, members of a drifting band. That is why those children inspire in those who watch them from outside a fear that is always a class fear. But there is more. For as much as the fear of street children is fear of the revenge which the intimidated mob will exact, it also contains a much more ancient fear, a fear of the smothered child – or oppressed woman, conquered native, or assimilated Orient – that will return again to haunt civilization in the form of evil.[10] When we meet the eyes of street children, what we see there is not only the revolt of the unrestrained child who devotes herself to evil the moment he is set free, but also the mob, which becomes an uncanny thing when it is set free. Here is the collapse of the romantic nationalist myth of the pauper child who in spite of the calamity suffered at a tender age succeeds in becoming a just, noble, good-natured human being. There an unrepentant child mob has taken the place of the big-little saviour child, the humble foster child, the silent serving girl, the tearful orphan, the luckless adolescent – in short, all the children of agony.

This is where Kemalettin Tuğcu's nationalistic love of the poor, Yeşilçam's stories of orphans with happy endings, and all the tales of humbled adolescents give way to page-three horrors:

the moment when, in the eyes of society, the victim becomes the criminal. Page-three journalism locates the uncanny in innocence in the same way that horror films about satanic children do. But the fear that accompanies civilization returns now on page three with a class content. There we find monstrous mothers, vicious fathers, families torn to pieces, lives extinguished; people whose lives are susceptible to murder and mayhem, who may kill or be killed at any moment – almost all of them from the lower classes. The horrors there are always the manifestation of some evil, low-class fate, a pathological nucleus the poor masses are somehow born with. Our fundamental discontent with the civilization into which we were born is there reflected in people who are always poorer than we are, worse than we are, and worse-off; the evil we know is in fact always with us is there relocated to an always extraordinary, fantastical and alien setting. In the same way that horror stories relocate fear to a distant 'once upon a time', to dim-lit locales far from civilization – corners of the world inaccessible by road, dark forests, mountaintops, lonely chateaux – page-three sensationalism bonds it to the dark nature of people always distant from us, to a satanic nucleus lying in wait within them which might jump out anywhere at any time, leaving us no recourse but tense expectation. With the one difference that here the identity of the murderer is known from the start; what is not clear is where and how he will spring into action.

This is the supernatural setting street children have bestowed upon us. Above all, they represent a world where the separation of child from adult does not quite exist. They possess a life-knowledge drawn from exposure to institutional evil – state oppression, the violence of the military, police brutality – at a tender age. But there is something else: for we who pass them by, street children belong to the realm not of suffering but of crime and transgression, as much by virtue of their knowing glances seeking out our wallets, not our consciences, as by virtue of their dull, expressionless faces on which we find it hard to see the précis of agony. What we see on their faces now is not the loveable street smarts of the child who saves his parents from dens of sin and iniquity, but proof that no child will ever be able to accomplish such a thing, and moreover that it is not that easy to rescue a family from disintegration, that some fathers are condemned to the prison, some mothers to the hospital, and some children to the street. And that is why they are not the metaphor of a national failure but the objects of a class fear compounded by fear of the revenge despised children will one day wreak upon adults.

It is enough to glance through the offerings on television. On one station we find one of those touching poetry videos drenched in portentous language, titled 'Street Child'. On another, a news announcer trying to seduce viewers with his 'street child image'. All of this shows us that if the adolescent sensibility fed on suffering is no longer quite credible, it still has its customers in Turkey. But the visions of street children which have destroyed the romantic image make clear to me that the 'child of agony' was a sleight of hand, not only because it prettied up suffering with an image of adolescence, and hid it behind the image of a child wronged but not damaged, but also because it concealed the fact that in Turkey society fears suppressed childhood as much as it does the intimidated masses. It is possible to create a romantic poetics of street children, but they will never symbolize a national feeling of abandonment, an Oriental orphanhood society can share.

It seems that Turkey will now find its popular heroes not in oppressed, victimized orphans who distribute justice in spite of all, not in vulnerable children of the East who act honourably despite the suffering they endure, but in a new young man type who has no need to see himself as innocent, the strong Turk full of rage, ready to commit crimes in order to rid society of its new objects of fear, ready to do anything to protect the city from filth and anarchy. At least for a while.

EIGHT

Bad Boy Turk (1)

I

AHMET HAMDİ TANPINAR's novel *A Mind at Peace* has one of the few anti-heroes in Turkish literature.[1] Although Suad is not the novel's main character, he is one of its important figures. It is Suad who, with his atheism and contempt for restraint as much as his vile, morbid nature, obliterates any possibility of contentment from the start and makes Tanpınar's *A Mind at Peace* a novel of disquiet. He is a dark soul who unsettles all with his emphasis on the material over the spiritual, his preoccupation with absence over presence, and his disregard for moderation in pursuit of his bizarre tastes. He reminds all who believe in cultural attainment or personal happiness that every human being ends up a hideous, rotting corpse. He believes that cruelty liberates a man from the cruel play of this world, and that the goodness in man is to be discovered by way of murder. From his sickbed at the sanitorium, filled with resentment at his illness and hatred for goodness and good health, he seeks to poison all around him. His wicked ways do not lack an impulse towards transgression. Suad will strike out with all the force of his defiance against both İhsan, the man of ideals, and Mümtaz, the man of dreams and aesthetic tastes; Suad, bored with social convention, ridiculing the mediocre ideas, moderate pleasures, measured compassion, small hopes and shallow sufferings of the intellectuals around him, will cast over the love novel we are reading a shadow of destructive emotion, malicious suspicion and rancour that neither love nor culture can conceal. Tanpınar called him a 'dirty hand': he will enter into each person's life 'like a dirty, sticky hand with filth dripping from its fingers enters a cupboard full of clean linens'; he will make of every thing 'a repulsive jelly', dragging everyone into that 'black, murky, virtually ashen mud'. Suad is likened plainly to shit: he will dirty everything with the 'disgusting leaven of his morbid, murky personality', smear everyone with that 'viscid heap'. In all these respects Suad deserves to be known as one of the few demonic and, for all that, miserable figures in Turkish literature.

A Mind at Peace tells the story of the love between Mümtaz and Nuran. But Suad has an essential role in the development of the plot; for it is he who, with his presence as much as his suicide, and that horrific smile on his dead face, succeeds in making Nuran regard love with disgust; he who leads Mümtaz into 'the sinister attraction of deadly things', drawing his attention to the underground of high culture, to the sort of people whose lives he will never understand and who have little place in this novel of ideas partly because no one has ever asked them what their ideas are. It is after Mümtaz comes under Suad's influence that his attention strays for a moment from his beloved Bosphorus, its mosques and seaside mansions, and he notices, even if just out of the corner of his eye, things his aesthetic gaze could never include. He realizes that there are streets where sewage flows out in the open, people who live in homes made of tin cans and mud bricks, apprentice boys working for coffee-sellers, porters carrying heavy loads in baskets on their backs, 'a humanity ready to tread upon all culture and manners'. Moreover, it is Suad who injects nightmare into Tanpınar's dream aesthetic, who breaks up the art–nature–love triangle of the novel, who undermines concepts like 'the dream' and 'the sultanate of spirit' which give the novel philosophical depth. Clearly Tanpınar used Suad to include in the novel things the aestheticism of Mümtaz does not record, in an effort to describe evil not as an external enemy but as a seductive, internal force.

And here is the problem. Despite his essential role in the novel, Suad is not a believable character; he even seems to be an imitation character in many ways. He is too literary, too symbolic, as if he were put there merely to represent evil. True, he gives us some distance on Mümtaz's aestheticism, and furthermore saves the novel from becoming a parade of ideas and reverie, but he somehow cannot be rescued from his status as a kind of copy, a foreign concept. At most he is the representation in the external world of Mümtaz's melancholy side, fed on death, exile and loneliness, the emptiness into which Mümtaz withdraws during the years following the deaths of his parents; Suad is that 'leaven of death' within Mümtaz, the external exemplar of Mümtaz's unhappy consciousness. It is as if he were put in the novel merely to undermine the meaningfulness of the cultural material Mümtaz crams into his inner world, to crack up the thick cultural layer there and point to the bottomless emptiness beneath; in short, more to authenticate the main character's anguish than Suad's own morbidity. Beyond this symbolic role, Suad is plainly foreign. This is made perfectly clear when he commits suicide while listening to a Beethoven violin concerto. Critics have persistently focused on how Suad is an artificial, borrowed character, an imitation, even a translation – that he comes out of Dostoevsky. His suicide in particular is too much like that of Stavrogin in *The Possessed*. According to critics, Suad's is a 'translated suicide'.[2]

II

The critics are not without a point. In one of his writings Tanpınar said, with reference to the cosmopolitan Istanbul district of Beyoğlu, that everything we find there has its 'truer' counterpart outside of the country. The same can be said of the character he created. Suad really does stand before us as a Russian–French–German literary hybrid. He is propped up with a little Nietzsche, a little Baudelaire, and a lot of Dostoevsky. Everything he says seems to be a repetition of something we've read elsewhere. In Dostoevsky, in German philosophy, in the French Decadents, and in the Italian Futurists as well; for Suad wants 'Virgin Turkish folk songs', he wants 'the newborn man to be sung of', he will not accept 'any leavings of the past', he believes that war is cleansing and that only through war will humanity be liberated from dead forms; he is in favour of tossing out Ronsard as well as Fuzuli. This man, who seems to be surrounded by Turkish taverns, Balkan folk songs and whirling dervish music in Ferahfezâ mode as the result of some sort of accident, really is exceedingly foreign. He stands dumbfounded before religious feast pastries, songs sung by drummers waking the faithful during Ramazan, printed headscarves from Kandilli and textiles of Bursa weave, in short 'the forms we have created in this land out of our own lives'; he is an *alla franga* evil composed of foreign ideas, a dandy scoundrel, an overly chic bad boy.

The interesting thing is that a similar accusation is levelled at Suad by Tanpınar himself, through the mouth of İhsan: 'What is sad is that', says İhsan,

> the entire world experienced this sort of torment a century ago, and used it up. Hegel, Nietzsche and Marx have all come and gone. Dostoevsky suffered like this eighty years before Suad did. You know what is new for us? Not Éluard's poetry nor Count Stavrogin's torment. What is new for us is a murder, a land dispute or divorce happening this evening in the tiniest Turkish village in the most far-off corner of Anatolia.[3]

Unlike the 'tangible' longings special to folk song, Suad's suffering is abstract, airy and borrowed. Tanpınar, who criticized Halit Ziya, an important novelist of the Tanzimat era, for being artificial and pretentious, not 'one of us', saying his works 'lacked the taste and warmth of something really ours',[4] seemed now to aim the same criticism at his own hero. Bad boy Suad is a belated hero even in the eyes of his own creator; he can never be more than a washed-out copy of foreign models because he is devoid of spontaneity and naturalness. Furthermore, there is an unintended irony here. For Suad – a wretch who claims it is imperative to tear away the dozens of cultural layers people use to bury the bottomless void within, a wretch incapable of making peace with any ideal, put there to destroy the contentment of people who live by ideals – to turn out in the end to be a mere concept; for Suad – who explodes, 'you live by words!' – to turn out in the end to be a word translated from another book; for the man who tells Mümtaz, 'You make up stories ... I simply live', to turn out in the end to be that 'well-known story' taken from a book, truly is ironic. That is what makes him less convincing than any other character in this novel of ideas. Alright then, but why? Why isn't Suad more than a statement of evil we recall from other books, a copy of evil that reminds us of other characters we know? Why does Suad, not for his critics alone but also his own creator, remain a fake imitation of foreign bad consciousness, someone else's bad boy?

I will discuss a linguistic obstacle first of all: Suad seems to have fallen into the wrong linguistic environment. Tanpınar's overly pliant, adjective-heavy, simile-ridden style, bearing all towards that 'sultanate of spirit' he loved so much, operating to forge a synthesis out of even the most disparate elements joined in harmonious statement, insistently calibrated to the beautiful and sublime, does not much suit the narration of Suad's bad consciousness. It seems to be this aesthetic of harmony itself, uniting the beauty of women, the Bosphorus and fine Turkish speech within the same broad fund of experience, the same broad poetry and orderliness of spirit, which creates a problem in the portrayal of Suad.

I am trying to say that in the same way all the urban and rural metaphors in *A Mind at Peace* (Bosphorus villages and ancient fairy tales, Trabzon folk dances and Bektashi hymns, Balkan folk songs and silver-thread embroidery), all the cultural forms of East and West (compositions by Dede Efendi and Wagner operas, mystical music in Ferahfezâ mode and the poetry of Baudelaire) stand side by side in the same novel without causing a rupture, so do all the old and new terms and native and borrowed words (obsolete Ottoman words, psychoanalytic and modern scientific terms, French and English borrowings) stand side by side in the same sentence without creating tension. Tanpınar can even move suddenly from the Trabzon hymn 'Rose' to Fra Filippo Lippi's painting of *The Infant Jesus amidst Roses*; he is able to combine the two along a single axis of the sublime as parts of the same broad fund of experience. The novel moves back and forth between dreams and disappointments, peace of mind and disquiet, spiritual sultanate and spiritual void, but when it comes to the abominable Suad, that jeering character who feeds on nothingness, that degenerate who belongs to a world which has long since lost all harmony, the limits of Tanpınar's diction have been reached. It cannot internalize negation, decay, disintegration or degradation. So, in order to describe that unwholesome, 'repulsive jelly', Tanpınar has recourse to a phraseology of evil taken from foreign texts. And then while whirling dervish music plays, our bad boy will suddenly talk like Stavrogin, and in the end commit suicide in a house on the Bosphorus to the accompaniment of a violin concerto played loud enough to drown out the sound of the call to prayer coming from the mosque next door. Tanpınar himself must have sensed towards the end of the novel that his diction of potentiality had become an impossibility. It is significant that at the end of the novel, while Mümtaz is again talking of Botticelli's angels and the Passion of Christ, Suad's ghost complains precisely of the simile-laden language that had besieged him: 'Enough of these meaningless comparisons... Can't you speak without likening one thing to another? Do you still not understand how much you have complicated things with those bad habits?'[5]

But perhaps the problem is less Tanpınar's aesthetic preferences, and the inadequacy of language to which they lead, than what he called 'the life of this country'. Şerif Mardin has said that the difficulty we encounter in adopting the word *daemon* in Turkish has a structural cause. According to Mardin, the difficulty demonstrates that here in Turkey, the dark side of a person constitutes 'an axis of human behaviour which has remained veiled' in modern as well as traditional culture. It is source of both the creative and destructive force in a person, and 'in civilizations where the daemon is not acknowledged, where it is masked and considered merely one and the same as "evil", literature and art are condemned to remain superficial.' Mardin maintained that this is why the genre of tragedy never developed in Turkey, why Turkish literature is impoverished, why the fantastic in Turkish visual arts is merely a formal imitation, and even why Turkish psychiatry is superficial. In his view, a civilization that tends to recognize the daemon only as an external enemy is doomed to superficiality, fakery, one-dimensionality and imitativeness when narrating the inner adventures of that hidden force. Turkish literature has mastered narration of 'the threat from without', but when the same story is narrated from within, 'an impasse' is reached, 'an artificiality, or at least a "stencil" style' comes into play.[6]

Here the problem of imitativeness confronts us once again in a broader cultural context. If Mardin is right, a demonic intellectual in Turkey and a demonic character in Turkish literature are to be sought in vain. If that is the case, then Tanpınar's 'cultural repertoire', like that of many other Turkish authors, 'leaves no opening for him to understand the daemon within himself', and that is why Suad is so bookish. If Mardin is right, perhaps that is why in, for example, the dozens of books published about Satan in recent years in Turkey, the material concerning 'Satan in Islam' is so lacking in any provocative charge, so boring, compared to the lusty 'Satan in the West' chapters.[7] Perhaps that is also why even when Turkish Satanists prove their seriousness in blood, they always seem to us to be imitating a project conceived in faraway lands. We feel the same way when we hear, say, verses from Baudelaire's *Flowers of Evil*, or a passage from Genet's *The Thief's Journal* read out in a bar in Beyoğlu. They are someone else's bad boys; when their rebellion against European parents is relocated to a different geography, it inevitably changes into a gesture, a borrowed mimicry. Tanpınar may have felt that as well, and so had İhsan kill off his character before others could: with his borrowed desires, belated torments and acquired negative ideals, Suad is alien to 'the life of this country', a bad boy who does not suit 'our bodily constitution', and so he will remain. If Mardin is right, if the *daemon* is all that is alien to this land, that is the conclusion we should reach.

III

Here I propose to carry to another level this debate which has been locked into dichotomies of East/West, local/imported, authentic/imitation, original/copy. I will say that imitation is the fundamental dilemma not only for Suad, but for all of literature's bad boys. I have said above that critics found Suad to be a 'translated' character; they maintained that he was translated from

Dostoevsky in particular. But if we do not rest content with that
first impression, and take a step further, we discover something
which pertains more properly to genre. This is the dilemma of
almost all of Dostoevsky's characters who venture into depravity. In *Crime and Punishment*, it is precisely this that Razumukin
tells his friend Raskolnikov, who claims that only extraordinary
people have the right to transgress the law, who commits murder
in order to distinguish himself from the docile masses, who sheds
blood so that he will not remain an insect like everyone else but
become a Napoleon: Raskolnikov wants to be different from
everyone else, but 'there is no trace of independence' in him,
he is at most 'a pale copy of a character from a foreign novel'.
What the police inspector Porfiri says is no different: 'You have
applied a theory, and when it turns out to have nothing original
about it, you are embarrassed.'

Crime and Punishment is the story of how Raskolnikov's murder
– a bloody deed committed in order to transcend the ordinary
and become a Napoleon – winds up in the end an ordinary
court case. Yes, perhaps Suad is a pale copy of Raskolnikov; but
Raskolnikov himself is like a character from a foreign novel;
even when he transgresses the law and sheds blood, he cannot
escape imitation, artificiality, falsity. Yes, Suad is a translation
of *The Possessed*'s Stavrogin; but at least at the beginning of the
novel the bizarre, arrogant, brazen Stavrogin, who challenges
common sense under the influence of repulsive sentiments, is far
too reminiscent of Prince Hal, whiling away his time with the
debauched Sir John Falstaff in Shakespeare's *Henry IV*. When
introducing Raskolnikov to the reader, Dostoevsky openly refers
to him as Prince Harry. Moreover it occurs to Stavrogin, while he

is confessing to Bishop Tihon, that the sufferings he has endured may be made up: 'Perhaps what I have said of myself really is a lie.' What most enrages Stavrogin is not that he is hated for the evil things he's done, but that he may appear laughable to those who read his confessions, that he may become an object of ridicule, and in a sense never be authentic. Furthermore, that problem of being 'alien to our bodily constitution' which plagues Suad is a problem for Stavrogin as well. Shatov says to him: 'You have lost your sense of good and evil, for you no longer know your people.' Dostoevsky clearly felt that there was an acquired aspect to Stavrogin's suffering: Stavrogin completed his studies in Europe and it is clear from the spelling mistakes in his 'Confessions' that his knowledge of Russian grammar is deficient. Yes, Stavrogin's nihilism may make him a stranger everywhere, but especially in Russia. He has long since lost his connection with his language, his country and his God.

Of Dostoevsky's anti-heroes the one who gives most thought to his own descent is set put before us in *Notes from Underground*. What drags down the underground man, who feeds drop by drop on his own spleen in his own underground, is wounded pride come of having been badly bruised at an early age and, along with the resentment which intoxicates him, his reaction against the utilitarian view that human existence is a calculable struggle for the greatest gain in life, a matter of progress towards nobility of soul under the command of reason. But his reaction is at the same time a rebellion against the transformation of his own existence into a banal fact explainable by statistics, economic formulas and scientific laws. What common sense and formulas and laws cannot explain, what makes him a human being rather than 'a piano key' or 'a screw', what makes him out of the ordinary and original, is his ability to curse at life. That is why the underground man sticks to his aimless wants, his irrational dreams, his vulgar desires: 'I would either be a hero or lie in the mud; there was nothing between the two for me.'

Here the dilemma of authenticity confronts us once again. Although the underground man says, 'No European measure can be applied to us Russians', as someone who has shed 'the essence of the land and the people' and got something from European culture, he is aware that he is doomed to be bookish, artificial and derivative even when he is cursing. And that is what drives him down. Liza tells him so at the end of the novel: 'You talk just like a book...' He himself admits it: 'My ruthlessness was so artificial, forced, so much a product of my own mind and out of a book that I couldn't stand my own behaviour even for a minute.'

It is as if a common literary fate has shaped both Tanpınar's and Dostoevsky's evil characters: the anti-hero who curses ordinariness, challenges common sense and transgresses generally accepted codes is in the end imprisoned in his own belatedness, his own derivativeness, his own ordinariness, with his ideas, desires and longings taken from books.

IV

We usually contemplate the idea of evil in connection with a primitive, untamable monster figure completely external to culture and bent on destroying it utterly. The monster is a representation of the rights of the body over the soul, of repressed sexuality, neglected gratification, destructive rage, and, at the same time, of boredom. But in fact the monster is never all that spectacular, all that unique, natural or alien to culture. It has a history; and for that reason is always belated. Here I will take a look at that belatedness through the history of the 'abject hero' with the help of the genre theory developed by the literary critic Michael André Bernstein.

In his book *Bitter Carnival: Ressentiment and the Abject Hero*, Bernstein speaks of how Bakhtin's carnival in fact internalizes a lament; for in literature the carnivalesque consists in remembrance of a tradition long gone. There are no footlights at a carnival; no distinction between spectator and actor, watcher and watched. But once we have spoken of literary representation, footlights have already come into play. According to Bernstein, belatedness is characteristic not only of post-Renaissance bourgeois culture but of an entire literary genre whose source lies in Saturnalian rites, with which Bernstein connects the birth of the abject hero also.[8] This degraded figure emerged as the polar opposite of the liberating power assumed to reside in the rites, the antithesis of the hopeful assumptions connected with them. In him the positive energy assumed to reside in the rites is transformed into negative energy. The abject hero is a mixture of the lazy, fat servant type who spoofs his master's weaknesses in Latin comedies, and the wise fool of Renaissance theatre. But he first emerges as a fully realized figure prior to the novels of Dostoevsky, in *Rameau's Nephew* by Diderot. Jean-François Rameau is the unhinged, incompetent nephew of France's greatest living composer; a musician himself, he is well educated, but has never been able to get out from under his uncle's shadow. He is a mean-spirited parasite who ridicules the Enlightenment *philosophes'* devotion to patriotism, friendship, civic duty and virtue as empty talk; he claims that the voice of conscience will always be drowned out by the growls of an empty stomach, and finds it more important than anything else to fling a crust of bread into a 'gaping mouth'; against the *philosophe* who defends virtue, he insists that the real issue is to be able to evacuate one's bowels freely in the evening ('O precious shit!'). Rameau is a shameless buffoon who would rather lead a depraved life on earth than rise above the clouds. In his personality are combined the servant with a growling stomach and the sad fool, abjection with a kind of sublimity, infamy with arrogance, and dishonour with an honesty rarely encountered. Not a magnificently satanic figure, he is more of a reprobate. On the one hand he ridicules the virtues and self-interests of society, and on the other adopts its most despicable qualities.

Bernstein's thesis is important: like the underground man who will follow him, Rameau's real suffering comes of being trapped in a literary-philosophical tradition.[9] What Rameau really fears, perhaps even more than poverty, is that others will not find him original ('I wanted to pull out of you the admission that at least I was unique in my degradation'); in other words, he fears being an ordinary example of his type ('A great scoundrel is a great scoundrel, but he is not a type'). Since he has failed to be an original musician, he must be an original parasite or murderer. But here again is the problem: no matter what he does, he cannot avoid adding another link to the chain that binds him, cannot avoid becoming a pastiche of everything he has said. According to Bernstein, the fundamental reason why Rameau or the underground man despises himself is that he realizes how much he lacks authenticity at the very moment when he most needs to feel original. It is in this respect that the abject hero departs from the Romantic monster, from the idea of an incomparable evil which severs him from all others; he is aware of his own belatedness, his own inventedness; he knows that he will always be partly an imitation. In order to overcome that belatedness, he sheds his fool's costume and begins to curse in earnest, to behave really monstrously, making a public display of his depravity so as to convince others that he is evil; but whatever he does he cannot avoid being a social parasite, and moreover a cultural parasite feeding off earlier texts. He is too theatrical, too belated, too derivative even as he curses in a rage. Thus as the fool in Western literature is transformed into the abject hero, degradation will be joined by resentment as long as he seeks his authentic voice; as long as he sees belatedness as an injury, he will be filled with self-contempt and self-hatred. What drags the underground man into resentment is not his lack of success but the fact that he cannot transform degradation into personal authenticity, that even his most personal rebellion is derivative, that he cannot speak without being indebted to Pushkin or Lermontov, or, worse, to Rousseau or Byron; even as he suffers he is aware that he is a literary cliché.[10]

The literary bad boy is usually a reaction against the mean, against moderation and common sense. Rameau wants to be 'a great scoundrel', 'original in his degradation'. Dostoevsky's heroes want to escape an existence as 'a flea', 'a bug', 'a screw', 'a piano key'. Suad wants to transcend tame pleasures, mediocre sensibilities, shallow sufferings. But the moment they try to achieve something uniquely, originally, extraordinarily evil, they are doomed to be a mere copy. In all of them evil appears to voice a drive which cannot be tamed by civilization – the growls of a hungry stomach, resentment at harm suffered at a tender age, destructive rage. It truly is a monstrous voice, but soon smothered in mimicry and gesture, quotation and cliché. Evil is always already belated when it is a matter of the literary representation. The bad boy is never natural enough, never instinctive or original enough; he can never be a uniquely evil man who blasts all around him with incomparable evil.[11]

The story Bernstein constructs around the characters of Diderot and Dostoevsky demonstrates that the abject hero is imprisoned within a literary-philosophical tradition; but there is an element missing which makes his analysis insufficient to explain the rage of Suad, at least. His haste to connect Diderot to Dostoevsky, *Rameau's Nephew* to *Notes from Underground*, the cafés of Paris to the underground of St Petersburg, to establish a continuity between the French parasite and the Russian reprobate, conceals an important difference: Dostoevsky's abject heroes are captive not only to a generic but to a national-cultural belatedness. There is a double belatedness here; while one cannot be reduced to the other, the former is always coloured by the latter. True, Bernstein says that in Dostoevsky a kind of social marginality has taken the place of the hunger pangs of Rameau, and that in the Dostoevskyan characters who shift back and forth between buffoonery and offence there are traces of a resentment particular to the idle, bitter intellectuals of nineteenth-century tsarist Russia. But because he stays within the limits of genre theory, we do not find there anything about how belatedness of genre is intertwined with cultural belatedness, how 'resentment against the world' is as much resentment against Europe as it is existential resentment.[12]

V

Orhan Koçak, in his essay 'Missed Ideal', wrote of how the Ottoman Turkish author was trapped in a double bind by 'that great paradigm drift called "Westernization" which is in fact *the acceptance of belatedness*'; that dislocation which transforms every effort into surrender right from the start. He is condemned to banality when he takes hold of the quotidian and local, and when he ventures into the realm of ideals he is dominated by foreign desire and awe. Once the world is viewed through Western ideals, there will be, on the one hand, local but prosaic, inadequate and ponderously unattractive content; on the other, a content which makes possible the generation of sublime ideals but is derivative; a lack of originality and naturalness, the superficiality and pretentiousness which comes of a subaltern position. 'On the one hand there is a foreign ideal which makes the other half appear banal and formless; on the other, a local reality which guarantees that the ideal will always be unattainable and appear to be fake.' According to Koçak, this double bind put authors like Halit Ziya, who was accused of aestheticism, on the same ground as their 'nativist' or 'traditionalist' accusers; both spoke from the same position of belatedness when confronted by the foreign ideal.[13]

Gregory Jusdanis voices a similar dilemma with regard to modern Greek literature: national literature inevitably emerges as a belated project in 'belatedly modern' societies. Modern Greek literature was born in an environment of both admiration and contempt for European culture, a desire to emulate as well as a fear of doing so; both responses are products of the same belatedness. The effort to create an autonomous aesthetic culture in which 'an imaginary realm where enervating dichotomies are harmonized and past battles forgotten' would play a role in Greece was as paradoxically belated a modern strategy as the effort to create a uniquely Greek literature.[14] So, we should speak of a double belatedness in the progress from Rameau to Raskolnikov or Suad. On the one hand, there is a generic belatedness which leads the author to feel that he is mimicking earlier texts even when he voices his most authentic feelings, and, on the other, a national-cultural belatedness which inevitably subjects his character to the domination of foreign ideals, making even his most authentic sufferings bookish, foreign and artificial. Both are intertwined inseparably in the case of Suad.

I have said here that the bad boys of modern Turkish literature were inevitably born into this double belatedness. But right away it may be asked: If all characters in Turkish literature are born into this bind, the good and the bad, what distinguishes the bad boys? First, it is in the bad boys that this double bind, and therefore all its dichotomies – spontaneity/mediation, authenticity/forgery, originality/imitation – are most apparent. For while the bad boy dreams of a spontaneous, unique wickedness that erupts out of nature, in the end he realizes how cultural is even the most natural action, how derivative even the most spontaneous behaviour, how belated even the most original emotion. Second, the bad boy is an answer to the trauma caused by the paradigm drift, the belatedness which begets the original/imitation dichotomy; but the answer to belatedness is itself fated to be late. Rather than oscillate between the two models, or somehow combine them, Suad aims to transgress utterly the confines into which he was born: 'Yes, to throw off in one step all that is old or new, toss it away. Neither Ronsard nor Fuzuli...' He goes even further: he sacrifices his own life, wiping out the subject of this belatedness itself. But it is precisely here that the bind returns; the shadow of imitation falls over even Suad's most authentic act, his suicide. Just as his suffering is belated, his suicide to the accompaniment of Beethoven cannot avoid being a 'translation'.

In fact it cannot be said that Tanpınar was unaware of all these problems brought on by belatedness; he made it felt here and there. While describing the relationship between Mümtaz and Suad, for example, he says: 'between them now, as a French poet put it, there spoke "the sinister attraction of deadly things".' While describing Suad he refers to Nietzsche, Marx and Dostoevsky. He too realizes that his character lacks naturalness, that he has 'joined the flowing river belatedly'. Tanpınar put into his novel all the conditions which degrade the abject heroes of modern fiction. With one difference: the voice of İhsan, who accuses Suad of living out a belated suffering, is never echoed in Suad's consciousness, not for a moment. İhsan's voice, coming from the realm of consciousness and will, and easy for the reader to adopt, remains a purely external voice in the novel. But Suad's problem is the problem not only of the novel's bad boy but of all its male characters. İhsan cannot talk about how one must have a 'personal identity' without quoting Péguy, or Shakespeare when speaking how the new Turk should behave, or Goethe when holding forth on the need for a culture 'particular to us'. Yes, Suad listens to whirling dervish music in Ferahfezâ mode as if he were a Russian or Frenchman; but all of the characters in *A Mind at Peace* who adopt a national or aesthetic ideal – İhsan, to the extent that he tries to create a national identity 'particular to us', or Mümtaz, to the extent that he seeks to achieve an autonomous aesthetic culture – share that inevitably belated ground. More importantly, to the extent that Tanpınar himself wrote novels synthesizing all these enervating oppositions into an ideal of the sublime, and tried to create an autonomous aesthetic in which all past conflicts would be forgotten, he occupies the same ground as his own bad boy. And perhaps for that reason, it occurs to me now, Tanpınar wanted to put Suad's belatedness out of the picture straight off. For it contradicts Tanpınar's idea of national identity as much as it does his claim to autonomy, his idea of creating a synthesis 'particular to us'. In fact what critics who find Suad unconvincing overlook is that he is unconvincing not because he adopts foreign ideals, or because he is a character out of Dostoevsky, or because he kills himself in a 'translated' suicide, but on the contrary because he is not sufficiently aware of his own inevitable belatedness, because he has not faced up to his inevitable derivativeness – that is, because Tanpınar could not have made that the stuff of his novel. That is why Suad had no internal voice. It is as if the author put him out of the picture early, as an idea 'which does not fit with our bodily constitution', because Suad too accurately mirrored it.

Şerif Mardin was right in saying that a genre emerging under specific conditions, a character type born into a specific climate of thought, is when it changes geography doomed to superficiality or insularity, at least at the start. But when that observation is repeated over and over again it points to a second: Mardin's criticism of imitation, or superficiality, itself bears the traces of the same bind. Turkish literature has been regarded through the gaze of precisely the foreign ideal we have discussed, and once again found wanting, fake and superficial. Once we have adopted Mardin's approach, the

Turkish intellectual, no matter how profound the knowledge with which he is armed, will not be able to go beyond 'neighbourhood manners' in his views on the subject of the 'daemon', and Turkish literature will never be free of melodrama.[15]

Yet one could very well have spoken of a belated consciousness, of a creativity nourished by having been born into that bind and a creative way to combine the belatedness of culture with that of literature; of an intermediate zone where 'destructive tension' becomes a creative tension, where the torment of belatedness is neutralized in literature's realm of play. Bernstein drew attention to how the figure of the abject hero in Western literature gained a creative voice to the extent that he became aware of his belatedness. He spoke of a dilemma pushing the abject hero into a doubled existence: now in order to be believable he must imitate a role which is in reality already his own, becoming the true charlatan of the condition that has made him a charlatan. It is here that Bernstein sought the reason why the Saturnalian dialogues were truly dialogic. For the abject hero who represented the impossibility of the Romantic monster, denied the glamour of a Promethean rebellion, found his place in the impossible realm where the satanic and the servile intersect. That is why his consciousness was a chamber echoing with unattainable desires and prohibitions. There the voices of the monster, the successful citizen and the famished parasite intermingle. Since a continually self-reproducing resentment could not be done away with definitively, the abject hero's constant conversation with himself dragged him into never-ending chatter and profound weariness with it. And strangely enough, it was here that the clichés dispersed and a more creative voice began to be heard.[16]

I will return one last time to Tanpınar. Yes, Tanpınar failed to create a believable bad boy in *A Mind at Peace*. But it was he who created the high ground from which later writers would gradually distance themselves, the plane of sublimity which made it possible for them to descend, and a linguistic register beautiful enough to allow in empty chatter, banality and malice. And an abjection similar to what we have described did not delay in making its voice heard in the Turkish novel of the 1970s. I am thinking of Oğuz Atay's characters. For example, the voice of Turgut Özben: 'There should be more vulgarity, human beings should become meaner as time goes on.' The voice of Hikmet Benol, whom Atay himself called 'a man of abjection', who 'returned to the evil ways of his childhood' and played evil tricks on people: 'I'm going to think of far-off evils to wipe out the ones right under my nose.' And Atay's own voice, oscillating between chatter and weariness ('I'm weary, Colonel, weary, weary, weary'). Where national belatedness ends, where literary belatedness begins – it no longer matters much. But clearly something is late; certain things were not said when they should have been, certain words are far too late, certain characters are long since out of fashion: 'Because I am someone from the past, someone long out of fashion', says Turgut, 'I am here by way of a representation.' Now the way to bring infamy to others is to bring infamy on oneself.

What debases Oğuz Atay's characters is that even when expressing their most profound hurts they know they are doomed to melodrama, banality and cliché. That the moment the footlights go up they sense that they are always already belated (Turgut: 'Everyone is here, they're watching us. Go away! We're not putting on a puppet show here. We are suffering.'); that like everything literary, literary evil, too, is mediated (Hikmet: 'But this is writing, dear Bilge, my wickedness gets lost in words'); that despite all their rebellion, they too are part of the established order (Hikmet: 'I rebel against the old order and I am against changing the old order. Ha-ha.'). In my opinion, right next to Atay's 'Don Quixote-like fate of supposing himself a knight because he's read too many romances' we should write down Vüsat O. Bener's sense of *sahtegi*-ness, what Bay Muannit Sahtegi[17] calls 'the chatter of unliberatedness'; and the 'wrong man' of Bener's *Ice Age Virus* ('Ah, what a wrong man I am, I'm ballast to throw out'). Like Hikmet's ha-has, Bay Sahtegi's boo-hoos bring us to an irredeemable sense of inauthenticity, the foolish, servile, scandalous character's derivative contents of memory. If not, why would Atay have spoken constantly of chivalric romances, underground men, possessed spirits, wounded Don Quixotes and princes of darkness? Why would Vüs'at O. Bener have constructed such a sentence as 'I was Knight Don Quixote with the face of El Greco in the music of Richard Strauss'? For me, the difference between Tanpınar's wretched Suad and these 'wrong men' is that the latter accept their belatedness and transform their own destiny – and that of the literature into which they were born – into the stuff of not only a belated literature but of always already belated literature itself. And that is what makes them believable in all their 'obstinate inauthenticity', their irredeemable artificiality.

I am not trying to say that the dilemma can only be transcended through worldly irony, just that this was one way to do it. There were others. For me, one of the most debased characters in the Turkish novel is Zebercet of Yusuf Atılgan's *Homeland Hotel*. Ridiculed by all, he possesses no diabolical force; unimpressive, puny, 'girlish', Zebercet is condescended to in the neighbour-hood, the whorehouse and the army. It seems to me that with this character who kills himself to the accompaniment not of a Beethoven concerto but car horns and factory whistles blowing during a 10 November ceremony,[18] whose unpremeditated act of murder is squeezed into a single sentence ('he suddenly leaned over and closed his fingers around her neck'), whose suicide is related in a short sentence cleansed of the 'meaningless similes' of *A Mind at Peace* ('he put the rope around his neck; he pulled it straight'), Tanpınar's student Atılgan tries to offer an answer to Suad's portentous, 'translated' suicide.

When we analyse the Turkish novel, let's say a little about what is there, not always speak of what is not. Let us record Oğuz Atay's unavoidable loss of altitude; Vüs'at O. Bener's banal, vicious, fake materials; Bilge Karasu's archaic, fierce contents; the harshness and dark of Leylâ Erbil; the suddenly apparent filth in Yusuf Atılgan's simple sentences, not just the sperm but the earwax and foot grime. Was not all that made invisible, spawning the judgement there would be no room in Turkish literature for darkness, by our insistence on viewing literature through the image of a satanic ideal, a unique romantic monster, a magnificent bad boy?

NINE

Bad Boy Turk (2)

I

THREE OR FOUR YEARS AGO I was in an Istanbul park when I heard boys shouting this bizarre slogan in the playground: 'Long live evil!' True, what they were doing at that moment was not unrelated to what they were saying. The boys, around thirteen years old, had given themselves up to mean impulses and were smashing toys with gleeful abandon, terrorizing the park designed for much younger children. Nonetheless, the slogan 'Long live evil!' seemed far too symbolic for the language of children, too foreign, too translated. Then I remembered it was something mouthed by a radio show host on one of the private channels. It was just a phrase, nothing too heavy; the meaner of a thousand and one buttons one could pin on one's lapel. Clearly the children had picked up on it because they were tired of the endless counsel of their elders to be good, bored with the insipid notions of goodness forced on them by parents and teachers.

Later I thought how this curiosity about evil, the uncanny and malign, is not always so childish; it does not always leave the impression of translation, and moreover the pull of evil has a symptomatic meaning in Turkey today. I realized how many of the character types in cartoon satire magazines in particular had for some time been based on an idea of evil. I had enjoyed some of these caricatures, and others not at all; there are cartoon strips called 'Cruel Şevki', 'Sheep Monster Orhan', 'Bad Girl', 'Evil Son Ökkeş', 'Crap Hamdi', 'Bad Cat Şerafettin'. It would not be fair to say they all follow the same line, or have the same message; there are many different voices there. Some have shown us that the ugly, brutish, dirty content neglected by an aesthetic of the sublime can be loveable also, and that a cartoon strip which does not ignore the local in Turkey can only be created by appropriating that homely content. In a polite world of mediocre pleasures and clearly demarcated lines, they speak to the part of us that wants to adopt social failures, freaks of culture and scrappy cartoons. Others – in an environment where most satirists see the local as a storehouse of the always already comic, and do no more than create caricatures portraying rural people maladapted to the big city as ever more ridiculous and unsightly – show that this manhandled local material could only be made attractive again by using a 'bad man' character type bolstered by the power of satiric gratification. By speaking for the elements society labels as 'evil', some cartoons made it possible for us to see that 'good' was an ideological construction also, and they allowed us to reverse the established symbolic meanings assigned to bad and good. Some used the language of evil triumphantly, trying to make a crack in the sheltered, indifferent surface of society. Others turned the malevolent energy of evil against itself, showing that not only suffering but laughter might come of it too. Some were a reaction against 'children of good family.' Others plainly prettified resentment as something cute. They gave voice to rage against power, but more often to resentment against the world of privilege, the well educated, and more recently against the urban woman portrayed as the representation of all privilege; a profoundly deep resentment armed as spokesman of local reality against foreign opportunity had all of a sudden been naturalized despite all the dilapidation of the cartoon strip genre.

Nor should it be forgotten that almost all Turkish television series, from *Black Angel* to *The Serpent's Tale*, from *Crazed Heart* to *Aynalı Tahir*, now feature a variety of evil rich characters. Diabolical, treacherous, snaky types; dark spirits who fall head-long into an abyss of evil upon a loss of moral fibre; malicious characters with piercing laughs, supposedly possessed of psychological depth, who scream 'bad people have a right to live too!'; men determined to do wrong, filled with resentment at old hurts; types who do bad things out of self-interest or just for the pleasure of it; black widows, bad guys using Oriental honour as an excuse, pathological monsters. After all the bland shows about happy families and loveable neighbours, these series show that society's curiosity has slid towards the dark and evil, at least for now. To be sure, there is always a rough-and-ready young man who vows to clean up the neighbourhood, but he too is locked into criminality, resentment and violence, at least as much as the rest. For long years Turkey chose beleaguered but good-hearted heroes, tormented but honourable, wronged but blameless, and defined itself as patiently resigned in the face of suffering; now the country appears ready to make use of its own store of roughnecks and hoodlums, even if cast in moulds smelling of translation from American series, ready to awaken the bid for power slumbering within its 'child of agony' and finally create its own bad boy.

II

In the first part of this essay I wrote of the dilemma faced by the bad boys of modern literature. They set out with the idea of achieving some incomparable wickedness by which they would transgress generally accepted codes, mediocre values and banal morality, shake civilization at its very foundations and separate themselves from the common herd. But in the end it is the bad boy himself who becomes a quotation, a literary gesture, a cliché of abjection. He hopes that uncanny emotions, pathological content and base impulses will come to his aid against mediocre ideas and false virtue, against insipid ideas of goodness which veil self-interest and the shallowness of an ordinary life lived for the sake of mere peace and security, but in the end he turns out to be nothing but a copy of evil characters created before his time. He seeks a singular, authentic voice, yet in the end is imprisoned in his own derivativeness, his own bookishness. But there I was trying to say that a literary bad boy can only become credible through his awareness of his dilemma. The abject hero escapes artificiality to the extent that he is aware he is imprisoned in a literary-philosophical tradition and in the culture he is determined to destroy. I was saying that the 'bad man' of Turkish literature achieves an authentic voice to the extent that he realizes his own belatedness, which has national-cultural as well as generic qualities. Now I would like to add something else to the discussion.

Martin Jay, in an essay titled 'The Uncanny Nineties',[1] discussed a contradiction inherent in the drift towards the uncanny
in both popular culture and theoretical thinking in Western
Europe and the United States. The uncanny was transformed
into a foundational metaphor, along with the related concept of
homelessness, in order to challenge totalitarian ambitions to re-
establish an ideal homeland presumed to have existed in the past.
But there is an irony here to which that metaphorical thinking
turns a blind eye. Recourse is taken to the uncanny as an antidote
to the quest for fantastical homelands, emphasizing how the
destructive content of the uncanny dissolves narcissistic ideals;
but this at precisely the time when more people in the world than
ever before have been left homeless, when a significant proportion
of the world's population has been forced to migrate and live
without a homeland. It seems to me that the literature of evil faces
a similar contradiction. Today the bad boys of fiction, poetry and
caricature, the abject heroes who would exemplify damnedness,
or boredom, are confronted by not only a literary-philosophical
tradition which makes clichés of them, or a subculture of evil
already sanctifying the damned, but a giant industry which, far
from suppressing the dark side, provokes people to revel in it;
an industry which makes plunder of evil and the uncanny, the
horrific and repulsive, and transforms all malign content into a
public display, a statement of chic, a cinematic special effect. And
perhaps more importantly, those in power in the world today carry
out their affairs in barefaced wickedness, piracy and thuggery
without even feeling the need for a credible ideology, however
false, couched in terms of any definition of the good. Today's bad
boy was born not into a sublime Good but into a world where evil

has been institutionalized, conventionalized and trivialized more than ever before. This particularly concerns the Turkish bad boy, child of a state which has long since lost its power to the West, a child forced to live with an inadequate but domineering father inclined to make up for his loss of hegemony by wielding a club. In a world where evil has made a profession of arms trafficking and drug smuggling aided by torture and assassination, where the horrific and the uncanny are so trivialized, how will that bad boy of ours employ the language of an incomparable evil in a triumphant mode? How should he believe that the malevolent energy of ostracization cannot be harnessed?

I think this is the fundamental issue for today's bad boy. Now that he is trapped here, how is he going to get out? How will he transcend the contradiction between an image of incomparable evil piercing the indifferent surface of the world and the reality that evil has already become a part of the collective madness produced by the system, the contradiction between the image of an uncontrollably savage monster and the reality that savagery can at any time metamorphose into the focal point of a disaster incorporated by the system? Today's Raskolnikovs are far too belated, both because they are already pale copies of characters in a foreign novel, and because they will become copies of perpetrators of page-three – or worse – front-page crimes; incomparable at first, yes, but fading in time. What can literature, politics or philosophy do, not only in Turkey but anywhere today, to get out of this bind?

TEN

'The Orijinal Turkish Spirit'

IN TURKISH CRITICISM it has become a reflex to begin by pointing to an absence. The critic opens with the indispensable statement, 'We have no philosophy', or 'We have no tragedy', or 'We do not have a novel', or 'We have no criticism'. Here is a criticism which takes its authority from comparison and derives the measure to be applied to a work from that comparison, rather than from the work itself. It manages to make itself credible by speaking of what 'others' have while 'we' do not, pointing to an irredeemable absence which demonstrates the inadequacy of its object right from the start.

To say that the problem stems from a discursive error alone would be disingenuous. For there is obviously something prompting the reflex, something which has made a reflex of criticism. We have dwelt enough on the belatedly modern society, the thought that accepts from the start its inadequacy in the face of a 'West' which imposes its superiority, a culture that feels itself in the position of a child when confronted by 'Western ideals'; it is all here. The paradigm drift generally called 'Westernization'; what the Greek-American critic Gregory Jusdanis calls 'belated modernity',[1] what the Iranian critic Daryush Shayegan describes as 'une conscience "en retard" sur l'idée"',[2] what the Turkish literary critics Jale Parla and Orhan Koçak have analysed as the sense of 'fatherlessness'[3] and 'the missed ideal'.[4] And it is that which has turned criticism into an art preprogrammed to speak of the great absence first of all. Especially with regard to the novel: because the novel is a genre which came to this land after the fact (say most critics), because its materials are second-hand, the characters in Turkish novels are not sufficiently believable, natural or original; they cannot avoid having imitation desires, copied sensibilities, bookish dreams. As if criticism had given up from the start due to a manufacturing error in the work; the critic is transformed into a Western observer who points out with the very first sentence the plenitude begrudged his subject, the richness and fullness there, 'outside', where all that is authentic resides. The object is primitive, childish and crude, and for that reason criticism just cannot surrender to it. The critic eyes his object from an always arrogant distance.

But we know that this approach has its polar opposite as well. If a first voice says 'We have no original thought, no autonomous novel, no characters of our own', a second says 'We have an authentic literature and thought of our own, deeper down, that's where we should look.' If the first devalues the object from the start with unconditional admiration felt for the foreign ideal, degrading the object as a shadow literature ('They have the good one, ours is a copy'), the second awaits the moment when the native self defeated by comparison, the forgotten authentic tradition, the autonomous inner world somehow untouched by trauma, will speak. 'Let us return to ourselves', it says, 'let us show the world how authentic we are'. I am not saying there are no other voices heard in Turkish criticism, but the general framework of criticism is laid out between these two poles, which, though seemingly antithetical, are in fact complementary. Criticism in Turkey is caught between snobbish arrogance and provincial pride, between xenophilia and xenophobia, between a cold gaze which throws the object's inadequacy before the foreign ideal in its face and the complacent warmth of nationalist indignation, nativism as authenticity, and slack Third World emotionalism.

Yet a well-intentioned gaze can make out behind these debates the desire for something genuine; the desire for an originary novel that would authentically record the tensions born of living in this land. Ahmet Hamdi Tanpınar was the author who gave voice to that desire in all its complexity, before it had become the originality reflex. In his 1936 essay 'Our Novel', Tanpınar asked why we do not have 'a novel of our own' and sought ways to ameliorate that 'great lack'. He attributed it to the absence of an expansive artistic life able to bear productive tensions; to a shortage of individual experience, or the problem of class; to the absence of a self-reflexivity derived from the Christian practice of confession, or to underdevelopment in the visual arts; most often he attributed it to a shortage of imagination among authors. Tanpınar's criticism was also comparative: he compared local examples to Western models and bemoaned the local's lack of originality. He was also the first to point out that the Turkish novelist's work inevitably suffered from a lack of vitality even when he allowed himself to be governed by the details of ordinary life, and lacked sincerity and warmth when he gave himself over to foreign horizons. So, the novelist is caught between a 'ridiculous and pathetic' nativism and a 'maimed, half-finished' model; either he kept to the West exclusively, or became 'a man of primitive tastes'. According to Tanpınar, both choices had spawned a mass of literary puppets devoid of depth.[5]

That dilemma brought Tanpınar to believe in the need for a literature 'completely ours'. He believed a literature having both human warmth and a horizon of aspiration, a literature no longer pathetic but not rootless either, would be born of an original synthesis with European ideals. Every statement he made about how such a synthesis might be brought about began with reference to something of 'ours': we must 'return to ourselves', create a literature 'appropriate to our bodily constitution'; we must 'be ourselves'. But the bind immediately makes itself felt: Tanpınar spoke of a national literature nourished by the national self, but even that statement was made under the pressure of an external model, in a desire to rise to its level, to win the admiration of the admired model:

> It is impossible that Europeans should like and admire us for what we have taken from them. At most they might congratulate us and pass on by. They will love us when we make known the things we have that are really ours; for then they will see that we equal them in bringing beauty to self-realization.[6]

Sixty years later Orhan Koçak considered the same double-bind within a psychoanalytic framework in his essay 'Missed Ideal'. When the Ottoman Turkish writer entered the arena of everyday life he was doomed to a nativism without ideals, and when he entered the realm of ideals he was governed by foreign desires, imitation dreams and borrowed ambitions. The first locked him into a prosaic world without horizons, and the second into one of subordination and pretension. The model drift called Westernization brought with it a doubled deformity. The ideal out there showed the local here to be shapeless; but the local had long since deformed the ideal. The ideal transformed the local into a slack, lumbering, primitive provincialism; but the local had already made a borrowed, half-hearted dandyism of that ideal. It really was a doubled deformation: the local became its own caricature, *alla turca*; but the ideal had become its own *alla franga* caricature as well. This, then, is the dilemma which still divides the literary world in Turkey, with writers on the one side regarded as pretentiously sophisticated 'snobs' while those on the other are seen as ill-educated 'provincials'. On the one hand there are critics who spy out imitation books, stolen plots and belated characters, reporting on what has been taken from where as guardians of originality; on the other hand there are critics who bemoan the lack of 'our own' warmth. Moreover, we know that the practice creates a head-spinning vicious circle. As a critic, Tanpınar found in the novelist Halit Ziya's characters 'a lack of zest and warmth due to the absence of anything really ours'; but later critics applied the same rule to Tanpınar as a novelist – Suad, the bad boy of Tanpınar's *A Mind at Peace*, was judged unbelievable because he was 'translated' from Dostoevsky.

Is there a space within literature where this bind can be transcended? Is there a space of ours, original to us, between Tanpınar's 'ridiculous and pathetic' nativism and his 'maimed, half-finished' ideal, between what Koçak called 'homely and

parochial' everyday life and the 'borrowed' foreign ideal? Is there
a third way between the arrogant criticism that views its object as
inadequate and the proud provincialism that speaks for a nativism
debased by the foreign ideal, between the condescending gaze
acting as spokesman of the foreign ideal and the angry nativism
Oğuz Atay[7] likened in his novel *The Disconnected* to 'neighbourhood kids throwing mud at children of good families'? If there
is, how should it be conceptualized?

In order to answer these difficult questions, I will try to re-
situate the concept of 'originality' itself within a problematic space.
It will be useful to begin by seeing the nationalist reflex in the
desire for originality. In the early years of the Turkish Republic,
the literary historian Fuat Köprülü asked the question this way:

> Why has the noble and orijinal [*sic*][8] Turkish spirit, which won the
> 'national victory' and created the 'national revolution'; that Turkish
> moral character kneaded by thousands of years of independence
> and sovereignty, which longs for freedom and abhors the slavery of
> foreign cultures, not yet entered into our literature? When will we
> attain the national 'masterpiece' telling us of the life and mysteries
> of Anatolia's pure and stainless Turkish people, and bringing our
> unconscious feelings into a conscious state?[9]

The Orijinal Turkish Spirit: the placement of the word *orijinal*
before 'Turkish spirit' in this phrase has made its dilemma felt
by now. The British literary historian Ian Watt pointed out that
the English term 'original' took on its modern sense at precisely
the time of the novel's emergence as a genre. In the medieval
period it meant 'having existed from the first', and underwent
a queer semantic reversal to acquire the meanings 'underived,
independent, first-hand' in the eighteenth century.[10] Although in

recent years the term *orijinal* has abandoned its place in Turkish in favour of *özgün*, it remained in use for many years and is still used today, in both of two senses. On the one hand, as in Köprülü's usage, it signifies a 'moral character', a thousands-of-years-old spirit; something not borrowed, subordinate or imitated, something which arises spontaneously from its own source. But on the other hand, it indicates something completely new, again as in Köprülü's usage, a 'revolution'; the independent, underived spirit of the newly founded Turkish Republic. It is significant that Köprülü used a word taken from Western languages to speak of that independent spirit. Yet it would not be correct to explain the dilemma here merely as a function of Turkish Republican ideology. For the insistence on the originality of Köprülü's statement above also lay behind the views of such an author as Cemil Meriç, who as one of the harshest critics of Republican ideals exalted sometimes the Ottoman of the past and sometimes a broader East, and at a date as late as 1980 wrote of the need to create 'an explicitly Turkish novel whose identity is loud and clear'.[11]

In this essay I am going to say that the insistence on originality is not, as has been supposed, the way out of the bind, but itself a part of the dilemma. I will say that all this emphasis on originality came about with the pressures which first created belatedness in Turkey, making some into snobs in awe of Europe and others into Europe-hating provincials. In order to deal with all of this, I will return to the prehistory of snobbery as much as that of the novel in Turkey. I will take a close look at *The Carriage Affair*, a novel which took as its subject the snobbery of the cultural climate into which it was born.

II

It has been said that realism in the Turkish novel began with a grotesque gesture; as Tanpınar put it, with a book sustained from beginning to end by one 'joke'. Recaizade Ekrem's *The Carriage Affair* tells the story of the *alla franga ʒüppe*[12] Bihruz Bey, an Ottoman aristocrat who falls in love with Periveş Hanım, a street tart he mistakenly takes for a fine lady. In fact Bihruz Bey falls in love not with Periveş Hanım, whose face he has never even seen, but with the fancy landau which carries her around, the district of Çamlıca where he sees the landau, Lamartine's poem 'Le Lac' (which the pool at Çamlıca reminds him of), and the operetta *La Belle Hélène*, which is playing there. And central to the pain Bihruz Bey feels at losing his beloved is another work of Lamartine's, written upon the death of the woman the poet loved, *Graʒiella*.

Tanpınar's views on *The Carriage Affair* are interesting. He said it was the first Turkish work to conform to novelistic structure; but he obviously did not like the 'transgressive realism' of the novel. He thought Recaizade had captured 'the comic', as far as that went, but indulged in exaggeration. The characters in the novel lived 'only externally, virtually like shadows'; according to Tanpınar, *The Carriage Affair* was a 'book of rootless shadows'.[13] In this grotesque comedy of errors which began and ended with a joke, it was the hero who most of all disturbed Tanpınar. Bihruz Bey was a 'not quite existent character' and Recaizade had not been able to give voice to his inner life. To be sure, one would not expect an organicist like Tanpınar, who insisted on cultural continuity, who took 'the inner man' seriously and never failed to mention 'our bodily constitution', to like a novel that was nothing but a joke. The novel really does tell the story of a *ʒüppe* made all of borrowed gestures, a shell of a man with no 'interior'. But this is what is so delightful about the 'transgressive realism' of *The Carriage Affair*: Bihruz's love is both the love of carriages and the love of texts. Without Rousseau's *La nouvelle Héloïse* and Lamartine's *Graziella*, without *Manon Lescaut, Paul et Virginie* and *La dame aux camélias*, Bihruz could not shed a tear, let alone fall in love. His inner world has long since been no more than an exterior – made up of clichés from the French Romantics, sensitivities taken from books and borrowed gestures. Tanpınar, who put our personal experience to the fore in his writings, who considered 'our bodily constitution' important, who claimed we must return to ourselves, arrived at the conclusion that *The Carriage Affair* was important only as the critique of a period, the story of a generation, or the psychology of an era.

Alright then, is that really the case? Is *The Carriage Affair* important because it is the novel of a passing caprice, an *alla franga* mode confined to the Tanzimat era? Is it no more than the critique of a period, the psychology of an era we have long since left behind? If there is an 'interior', where shall we look for it?

III

Bihruz Bey, with his shaky French, his disdain for Turkish, his alienation from Ottoman values, his unconditional admiration for Western culture and obsession with the order of consumption brought on by modernization, was a typical *alla franga züppe*. But *The Carriage Affair* is not the only work of Ottoman Turkish literature to spoof that figure. The character type first appeared with Ahmet Mithat's novel *Felatun Bey and Rakım Efendi* and was brought to us later again and again in several novels, among them

Hüseyin Rahmi's *Drop-Down Love* (Şıpsevdi) and Ömer Seyfettin's *Efruʒ Bey*. Şerif Mardin, in his article 'Super-Westernization in Urban Life in the Ottoman Empire in the Last Quarter of the Nineteenth Century',[14] explains the profusion of *ʒüppe*s in Tanzimat literature as the 'Bihruz syndrome'. According to Mardin, the profusion of such figures reflects the antagonism towards the *ʒüppe* characteristic of Tanzimat literature. The antagonism itself was a reaction to the shock Western civilization created in the Ottoman Empire. It gave voice to the reaction of the man in the street against the ruling elite, the Muslim neighbourhood against the showiness of Çamlıca, the traditional community against the sinful pleasures of the European quarter of Beyoğlu. It expressed the discontent of the communitarian lower classes with the market economy and personal consumption related to it, which they saw as threats to the traditional order. Bihruz antagonism was a new form, directed at the new elite, of the taunting ridicule which the shadow-play puppet character Karagöz, man of the people, practised on the pretentious charlatan Hacivat and his recondite speech. Ridicule is an aspect of social control applied to those who do not conform to the norms of the community; it was a way of ostracizing the super-Westernized elite which seized the reins of the modernization movement and turned its back on the people in their baggy *şalvar* trousers and *peçe* veils. So the 'Bihruz syndrome' reflected the passion for material aspects of Western civilization', on the one hand, and the communitarian reaction branding that passion as sinful, on the other.

The *ʒüppe* was a stock figure of not only Tanzimat but also early Republican literature: a good many novels revolve around the figure, among them Yakup Kadri's *Sodom and Gomorrah* and

Peyami Safa's *Fatih-Harbiye*. Furthermore, ridicule of the *züppe* plays an important role in political discourse as well. Many Turkish idioms carry a related charge: 'sweet-water Frank', 'salon social-ist', and even *entel*, short for 'intellectual' and an indispensable term in contemporary satire. The *züppe* is the polar opposite of martial manly virtue, street and neighbourhood sensibility, and community feeling. Mardin also says that the posture of Bihruz antagonism reappeared in that form of opposition to socialism in Turkey which lasted up until the 1960s. The same reactive stance can be traced in Turkish nationalism and in chauvinistic antagonism towards the West. Perhaps more important is the fact that it took writers of very different literary persuasions under its influence at the same time. Both Ahmet Mithat – a descendant of shopkeepers who favoured 'pure Turks, blessed Muslims', thought art for art's sake was a luxury, and usually worked themes of thrift, resignation and hard work in his novels – and a writer he accused of 'decadence', Recaizade Ekrem – known for his familiarity with *alla franga* comforts and one of the first to defend 'art for art's sake' – both ridiculed the *züppe* with the same ease.

Mardin connects Recaizade Ekrem's *züppe* antagonism with his sympathy for the Young Ottomans. The Young Ottomans were part of the elite who had not enjoyed the benefits of the Tanzimat to the full, were not happy with the speed of social mobilization in the modernization period, and believed a populist critique necessary to rally the masses to their political goals. They used for their own ends the discontent felt by the lower classes for the new values, and manipulated *züppe* antagonism in their struggle against the higher bureaucracy by accusing the men of the Tanzimat of creating a new aristocracy and forgetting the man in the street. In this way they aimed to mobilize the people in a more conservative mode around their own limited modernization project. Unlike the spontaneous Bihruz antagonism of Ahmet Mithat, theirs had an instrumental aspect. For the Young Ottomans, proponents of modernization themselves, Bihruz antagonism was an instrument to be used to sway the masses. Thus it became a component of traditional culture shared by the upper and the lower classes; Bihruz antagonism was a product of the distaste both the community and the communitarian Ottoman men of state felt for Western-style consumption.

IV

All of this explains why the *züppe* appears so frequently in Tanzimat literature; it explains why Recaizade Ekrem decided to write an antagonistic Bihruz satire, and even why Tanpınar felt Recaizade had no 'interior'. Yet as long as sociology does not problematize is own point of view, there will be an aspect it leaves unexplained: what makes *The Carriage Affair* different from other Tanzimat *züppe* literature is not that it makes use of communitarian values to satirize the *züppe*, but that it does not manage to succeed as satire, and perhaps does not want to. In satire there is something true, which the writer relies upon in order to ridicule his subject; he shows how pathetic, homely and silly his subject is, and the writer's voice is confident of its truth, decisive and net. But that is precisely the voice which *The Carriage Affair* lacks; there is no reliable narrator capable of judging the fool Bihruz. The authorial voice there is wavering; it shifts back and forth between third-person singular and first-person plural narration. More importantly, it sometimes uses Bihruz Bey's *alla franga* vocabulary to describe the world; it is not sufficiently distinguished from the voice of the hero it lampoons. It is that voice which makes *The Carriage Affair* not a satire, as it is generally called, but the novel of an author who has lost his voice. The novelist somehow cannot serve as guardian of reality, for the language that would ensure him that role is not there. Bihruz's *alla franga* diction, and the 'high' diction of the first generation of Tanzimat writers, and the diction borrowed from the French Romantics, and Ekrem's realism-seeking voice, all exist side by side in the novel. But that is precisely *The Carriage Affair*'s subject. Bihruz spends his life translating one language into another; he translates Rousseau, but 'the inadequacy of the Turkish language' does not permit him to; he wants to translate a lyric from the divan of Vasıf, 'the Béranger of the Turks', but Vasıf's Ottoman Turkish verse is as alien to him as Chinese; he can't understand even one line without the help of Sir James Redhouse's Ottoman dictionary. All of this makes *The Carriage Affair* not a satire but rather, as Jale Parla has shown in her detailed stylistic reading, a text comprising 'blind alleys of meaning, no-exits of communication, and strategies which increasingly disown their own text', symbolizing 'the literary crisis of the period'.[15] Recaizade's novel symbolizes not the *züppe* antagonism based on traditional communitarian values but the unavoidable literary crisis of the Tanzimat author who could only move forward by continually translating modernist principles into communitarian values, and the inevitable breakdown which emerged as a result of the comparison.

It may broaden our horizons to ponder that 'inevitable breakdown'. Unlike the previous generation of Tanzimat writers, Recaizade Ekrem kept out of politics, despite the sympathy he felt for the Young Ottomans. We know that he was one of the first to defend 'art for art's sake' when it was considered a luxury, and he took little interest in Arabic and Persian literature, again unlike the previous generation of Tanzimat writers; he was more influenced by French literature and represented the modernists in literary debates of the period. We also know that in later years he founded the Servet-i Fünun movement, which was accused of being artificial, rootless, and cut off from real life. All of this is, I think, is sufficient to show that Recaizade suffered from *Bihruzism* himself. For, like Bihruz Bey, he loved *alla franga* literature; he translated the novella *Atala* by Chateaubriand, one of the founders of Romanticism, and wrote a play based on it; he was influenced by Alfred de Musset and wrote the touching love story *Muhsin Bey* after reading Lamartine's *Graziella*; possibly he titled his book of poems *Tefekkür* (Meditation) because he had liked Lamartine's *Méditations*. Like Bihruz Bey, it was under the influence of the French Romantics that Recaizade came to love 'sad and touching things', as Tanpınar put it, and wrote about 'emotional and tragic' subjects. Ekrem was a writer under the influence of 'ideas infecting the age like jungle fever', according to Tanpınar, 'a man subject to all influences around him', a man 'lost because he had changed his trajectory'. He fell victim to a crisis of taste, writing vapid, belatedly Romantic poetry with an extravagant emotionalism learned from French books; childish, mushy works full of theatrical gestures, uncontrolled enthusiasm and empty sensitivity. If that is the case, Ekrem himself was a shell of a man. Speaking of Recaizade's *alla franga* ways, Yahya Kemal summed up: 'Ekrem Bey is *The Carriage Affair*'s Bihruz Bey, and there's an end to it.'[16]

That is precisely what I am saying in this essay: it was not easy for Bihruz Bey's creator to externalize his own inner Bihruz. The man who jokingly called himself 'Le Ekrem' must have sensed the truth in his jest; he must have seen when he looked within that his inner world was already made up of romantic clichés, exaggerated similes and borrowed phrases, and realized that his passion for writings novels came from his desire to be the other. It is generally said that the Tanzimat novelists were unable to turn their gaze within, and so mooched characters from Western novelists, filling their books with a mass of puppets utterly alien to our spirit. But now we must ask this question also: what if that was in fact what they saw when they looked within? What if what gazed back at them was someone else – yes, malformed, warped, maimed perhaps, but someone else? What if 'interiority' were a continuous process of external trauma, an exteriority? What if the inner world were not a naturally formed deposit which has always been there, but a malfunction? What if inwardness were a crowd of uninvited guests, 'ideas infecting the age'? What if experience itself were loss of experience?

We don't know if Ekrem asked those questions. But it is not easy to speak of 'our bodily constitution' in a country rushing to translate French classics and the works which served them as models into Turkish, bustling in haste to acquire as soon as possible countless classic works of world literature, from French to Ancient Greek and Ancient Greek to Sanskrit. The realm called 'the self' had already been transformed into a roar of discourse, a parade of books, a war of models. Recaizade Ekrem must have sensed, however faintly, that if realism was what he was aiming for, he himself was too much a part of the *züppe* problem to get off with a conventional satire. Clearly both the author and his character were swept up in the same flood; they longed for the same things and slammed into the same obstacles. We should not forget that for the Tanzimat writer, carriages and novels symbolized the same foreign ideal, the same order of consumption, the same modern life. What carriages were to Bihruz, the novel was to Ekrem. Just as Bihruz fell in love with a woman because he liked her carriage, Recaizade Ekrem fell in love with the novel because he was captive to an image of modernity. Here we find the carriage – dubbed *objet-roi* by Henri Lefebvre,[17] the 'king-object' as much a sign of consumption as guarantor of the consumption of signs – symbolizing, like the novel, the potential for a person to become the other, and, in a sense, the bridging of the gap between the centre of desire and its periphery. Or let us put that the other way around: the novel, like the carriage, is the promise of another life. Just as the carriage allows Bihruz to get out of his old neighbourhood, the novel allowed Recaizade to get away from the old Turkish literature he saw as a mess of homely speech and step into the world of Lamartine, Rousseau and Musset. All of this makes *The Carriage Affair* a text pointing to the inescapable *züppe*ry at the root of the Tanzimat writer's love of the novel: a parody of the Tanzimat that conveys the literary crisis of the age as it ridicules mimicry of the West, a black comedy that gives away its own inescapable *züppe*ry as it ridicules that of Bihruz. In *The Carriage Affair*, *züppe*ry signifies not only a condemnable excess but an impossibility exposing the fundamental character of the bizarre creature called the Tanzimat novel. And the time has come to expand the discussion further: *The Carriage Affair* is important not only because it provides us with the occasion to consider the inescapable *züppery* of the Tanzimat but the *züppery* anxiety in 'the *orijinal* Turkish spirit', and the feverish haste for originality there as well. For me the view of *The Carriage Affair* as satire is wrong because it locates both the novel's author and the critic who pronounces upon these subjects in an autonomous realm where *züppery* does not tread, putting the critic's own inescapable *züppery* beyond question, and regarding the novel as something much less than it is, regressing it to the status of a mere cautionary tale.

In fact Tanpınar understood this. He realized that the hero of *The Carriage Affair* was a 'not quite existent character', but backed away precisely because he realized that a spiritually sound authorial voice which could offer a contrast to Bihruz was also. Tanpınar favoured a diction nurtured on the luminous moments when the language of inwardness coincides with the language of a culture. He favoured a broad, rich, meaningful diction by which we might arrive at our own souls when we opened ourselves to culture, and find that culture when we looked deep within our souls. He always described the national synthesis to be made of Western ideals and local values as a bodily structure, a national body, a harmoniously functioning, living organism. Recaizade Ekrem spoke of something downright weird: foreign dreams had so deformed local characteristics, and local dreams so deformed foreign dreams, that there was no turning back. The inner world of Bihruz was plainly manufactured (*fabrike edilmiş* in Recaizade's *alla franga* Turkish). Moreover, not only the novel's hero but the novel itself was a freak spawned by the joining of two epistemological systems impossible to reconcile.[18] Tanpınar favoured totality, even if it were founded on escapist fantasies; he longed for the wholeness of the past and insisted on an aesthetics of harmony that could reproduce it in art. Recaizade established the comic on the ground of the impossible; he made us sense that the past might now consist of no more than a dictionary (and one compiled by an Englishman at that), that wholeness might be patchwork, that any synthesis made would inevitably be malformed. Tanpınar gave importance to 'the inner man'; Recaizade made one think that this 'inner' might be made up of external pressures. 'Return to yourself!' said Tanpınar. Reciazade made one think it might well be too late for that.

I think he was right. One can't return; for what is known as the self emerges as otherwise through always changing lenses, sometimes as a defensive reflex, and usually coalesced with a will to power. It emerges as national pride or resentment ('let us return to ourselves and show them what we're really made of'), as a effort to please foreigners ('let's return to ourselves and show them what we really are, that's the only way we'll get a Nobel'), at best as a decorative effort ('let us put something of our own into our works, something really Eastern'). Especially this last intimately concerns literature in Turkey today. For as long as 'our self' is not problematically defined, it remains a past effect merely for show, a few Ottoman motifs, an Eastern atmosphere. It is always too late to return to oneself. And more: the call to return is itself an expression of that belatedness.

V

Jules de Gaultier wrote his renowned *Le Bovarysme*, based on Flaubert's *Madame Bovary*, six years after Recaizade Ekrem wrote *The Carriage Affair* in 1896.[19] In Gaultier's analysis, characters afflicted with Bovarism lack naturalness and bow to suggestions coming from those around them rather than from within. Flaubert's characters have no 'originality of their own'; in themselves they are nothing and identify with an image they put in the place of the self so as to escape their own inadequacy and see themselves as they are not; they perceive themselves as other. All of this shows how problematic originality had become by the nineteenth century, and is important because it indicates the kind of world the novel was in fact born into from the very outset. For the novel begins where spontaneous, autonomous, unmediated nature is lost; at the heart of a second nature, woven of external promptings and foreign cultural codes.

René Girard made use of Gaultier's Bovarism theory in his *Deceit, Desire, and the Novel*,[20] written as a rebuttal of the Romantic thesis that imitative desire pales in comparison to original desire. Snobbism has an important place in the book. According to Girard, the snob who is a slave to fashion and desires only what others desire is an exaggerated caricature; but while his outlines are exaggerated, he brings the imitative nature of desire – of a lover's desire, or a child's, for example – to light in all its nakedness. The fundamental thesis Girard put forth, in a discussion ranging from Proust's snob to Flaubert's characters dominated by external suggestion, from Stendhal's arrogant characters to Dostoevsky's underground man, is constructed upon snobbism: to the degree that great novels tear down the absolute distinction between self and other – that is to say, the illusion of the autonomous self – they show us that we are no strangers to the snob's desire.

Girard's theory is powerful where he points out the moment when critical discourse is alien to the truth of the novel, arguing against that mode of reading which regresses the novelistic work to the romantic. Desire is not, as the Romantic critics assumed, natural and spontaneous, autonomous and original. The great novels exposed its mediated nature; desire includes the mediation of a model, the desire of another, and the desire to be the other. The nineteenth-century novelists Stendhal, Flaubert, Proust and Dostoevsky made clear that the 'internal' garden, which critics could not praise enough, was not as 'solitary' as had been supposed. They pointed to the dynamic relationship between individual desire and the structure of the collective, and revealed that the dialogue between self and other could be characterized by hatred as much as by desire. Girard showed how bizarre was Western critics' exaltation of the originality of Don Quixote, the imitation of an imitation, and their praise of Dostoevsky's underground man as a figure of spontaneity. This type of criticism, Girard said, gave expression less to the originality of the novel than to the lie of autonomy in modern man's desire to distinguish himself from the other and his tendency to forget the role of the other in his desire. The novel goes deep to the extent that it 'leaves behind the inner romantic', abandoning a mechanical opposition between self and other to bear witness that inner life is always already social. It is where the insistence on seeing desire as spontaneous and singular, the 'romantic pride' that makes us feel we are autonomous, breaks down that the truth of the novel begins. Romantic pride is the tendency always to see an autonomous, spontaneous, natural inner child in ourselves and an imitative, artificial, theatrical snob in others. In the destructive rage felt against snobbery, the feverish haste to reduce it to an excess worthy of ridicule and get rid of it, there is an effort to construct one's own autonomy. In order to conceal the role of mediation in the making of his own desire, a person gleefully exposes the existence of the mediator in the desires of others, ridiculing snobbery as an insipid flaw special to them. Yet the snob enrages us according to the measure of our own snobbery. We are enraged by the caricature of our own desire we see in him because we desire to be someone other than we are, and our desire is always frustrated.

It is no coincidence that Girard based his theory of the imitative nature of desire partly on Cervantes but mainly on the nineteenth-century European novel. When it comes to universal desire, the power of his theory comes from the fact of capitalism's creation of a single universe of desire. All of these novels were shaped by a center–periphery ebb and flow within which the laws of desire were universalized; not only capital and property, thought and ideology, but desire and longing spread without respect to class or country. This was the period, as Franco Moretti has shown, when desire outstripped need as the centre shifted from London, 'workshop of the world', to Paris, the 'centre of desire' where money could buy everything.[21] Girard places a similar emphasis on the location of imitative desire within a modern era founded on the principle of equality, not on brute force, violence or arbitrary power; an era when differences between persons are erased and everyone imitates everyone else. To all of this should be added a new type of reader who contributed to the formation of the novel: a reader who adopted the desires of others as his own and was ready to put himself in the place of others, a reader universal to the extent that he lived in a similar universe of desire. Both Flaubert and Recaizade kept *Graziella* by their bedside now; and Bihruz is reading *Paul et Virginie* just as Emma Bovary is.

Still, one cannot overlook the inequality lurking behind that universality. We are speaking of capitalism here. As most of us know from novels, and also from our own personal lives, the journey to desire that novels relate – even in the romantic reversals where the savage rural, the noble savage, the innocent child, or the enchanted East is an object of longing – is always a journey from the lustreless countryside to the shining metropole. Desire follows capital: it sets off for the homeland of capital in pursuit of new goods, shiny objects, dazzling possessions. Bovarism and Bihruzism coincide at the moment when the French woman and the Ottoman aristocrat are both dragged into conspicuous consumerism. *Madame Bovary* is the first 'tragedy of the consumer';[22] once having learned of the latest Paris fashions from popular novels, newspapers and magazines, Emma must buy the latest products from Paris in order to realize her desires. Just as the reader of *Madame Bovary* is impressed less by Emma's emotions than by the pools with soaring fountains, silver candelabra, silk curtains, satin slippers and fine wines in delicate glasses she longs for, so is the reader of *The Carriage Affair* impressed less by Bihruz's emotions than by his walking cane with its silver bob, the enamelled watch in his waistcoat pocket, his shiny patent leather shoes and the brand name embroidered in the lining of his chic coat. Is it a coincidence that the central theme of *The Carriage Affair* is a sub-theme of *Madame Bovary*? One of the desires Emma keeps most secret is her desire to possess a blue carriage drawn by English horses. Just as what defines Bihruz is his displacement from traditional Süleymaniye to chic Çamlıca in a landau, what defines Emma is her displacement from Yonville to Paris in a coach. Like books which arouse passion, carriages bring the countryside nearer to the centre of desire. Flaubert's early writings are full of interiority; he was swept up in the general craving for sentimental novels of love like his heroine Emma; Recaizade composed a great deal of sentimental poetry before he wrote *The Carriage Affair*; and it is perhaps only in the parallel between the two authors' development that the interior-less Emma resembles the interior-less Bihruz. But it is no casual resemblance.[23]

I said that modern desire follows capital. Is it not the distance of the periphery from the land of capital which makes it peripheral? That is why there is no rural sufficient to itself, no rural to which one can return. Not in Turkey, or anywhere else. The rural is not a far-off pastoral land or self-sufficient countryside, as trashy novels and advertising posters would have us believe; it is that which has been provincialized. The provincial is by definition a degradation which cannot occur spontaneously. Characters in novels who are prisoners of external suggestion lose their spontaneity because they have been captivated by that seductive light. Emma Bovary loses her originality because the characters in the novels she reads hungrily all night long are like 'shooting stars' in the dark night of history, and the touch of that burning light by way of books has opened a wound in her life that will not heal. Here the paths of Bovarism and Bihruzism cross once more. Just as Emma sets her sights on Paris because she had 'the dust of cheap books on her hands already at fifteen', Bihruz sets his sights on Çamlıca because he is besotted by the operetta *La Belle Hélène*. Even the dreams of the French woman and the Ottoman aristocrat are populated by the same book: as a young girl in the convent Emma reads of the love between two pure hearts set against the background of virgin nature in Bernardin de Sainte-Pierre's *Paul et Virginie*; Bihruz Bey reads the same book just before he falls in love. Many novels have been written about how that light, whether emanating from books or other quarters, transforms lives into a rural to which there is no return. The moment that light strikes Emma, her unenchanting husband becomes insipid in her eyes. Even nature suffers its blight: as descriptions of the snow-covered mountains of Switzerland give Emma's soaring spirit a sense of unbridgeable distance, her own garden becomes a spirit-deadening, vulgar thing. It is most of all here that the national-cultural difference comes into play. For Bihruz Bey it is language itself which becomes insipid most of all, not merely his old neighbourhood or the natural scenes that surround him. All of a sudden Turkish becomes a language incapable of expressing sublime emotion: Bihruz's effort to express his love remains frustrated by 'the inadequacy of the Turkish language'.

It is here that the fates of the snob and the provincial coincide. To be provincial means to see oneself through others' eyes as primitive, inadequate, childish; it is nothing else but this inadequacy that the snob who longs to be someone else hides. What novels have shown us is that the snob and the provincial are less polar opposites than figures capable of becoming one another. As Girard put it, Don Quixote is nothing but a snob in the eyes of the village nobles. The people of Yonville must also have seen Emma as a snob. When we excavate the snobbery of Bihruz, we find the orphaned Ottoman banished to the provinces of the world. It is from this point of view that we should consider the seductive call to return to an originary Turkish self, the preoccupation with the two exaggerated types and feverish haste to expel them from 'our bodily constitution'. They are dreary caricatures, these two, and they define our structure; contrary to what is supposed, each can change into the other, all of a sudden.

VI

The genre of the novel began with the story of a lunatic nobleman whose mind had been so deranged by reading chivalric romances that he saw the world around him through those books. It is no accident that *Don Quixote* found echoes in Ottoman Turkish as well as European literature. The history of the novel has since *Don Quixote* been filled with countless characters who misunderstand the reality of the world around them because they live in a world of borrowed desires; countless characters who seek an original voice yet realize they are doomed to mediocrity. And that is the trauma: in *Crime and Punishment*, Raskolnikov longs to be a Napoleon; he spills blood to separate himself from the ordinary crowd, but in the end realizes that his crime is no more than an ordinary court case, and he himself 'a faded copy of a hero in a foreign novel'. In *Notes from Underground*, the underground man is disgusted with life – which he learns about from books – and rains down curses upon generally accepted norms, common sense and mediocrity; but in the end he understands how false, how artificial, how borrowed from books those curses are. In *The Possessed*, Kirilov chooses death, 'daring to desire nothingness', in order to defy God; but even his death is a mediocre imitation of the death of Christ. In Tanpınar's *A Mind at Peace*, Suad defies the mediocre ideas, measured pleasures and calculated sympathies of the intellectuals around him and kills himself in order to take revenge on them all; but his suicide to the accompaniment of Beethoven is an imitation, and he himself a reflection of Dostoevsky's Stavrogin. In Oğuz Atay's *The Disconnected*, bookworm Selim cannot grow up because he confuses life with books; he exhausts himself trying to be Dostoevsky, Gorky and Oscar Wilde all at the same time and dies young, a suicide.

'I read a book and it changed my life': readers responded so enthusiastically to the first sentence of Orhan Pamuk's *The New Life* because it gave voice to the fate of the novel itself as well as that of all its bookish characters. The novel emerged with a claim to originality; it would take its subjects from personal experience rather than from history, mythology, fable, legend or older literature. Its value as literature would be determined not by its conformity to older models, conventions of form or lack thereof, but by its fidelity to personal experience. For that reason its English name means 'new'; for that reason the word 'original' acquired its modern meaning ('underived, independent, first-hand') as the novel came into being. As long as the novel remained faithful to experience, authors would be able to make whatever use of previous genres they wished.

And that is where the problem I have discussed in this essay began: in order to be original, the novel had to remain faithful to singular, local and completely new experience; but in a world where ideas spread like epidemics, where desires are contagious and passions infectious, experience itself somehow cannot be authentic; it is always confronted by the problem of belatedness. If this is the truth of experience, then to remain faithful to experience is also to be faithful to the experience of a character who somehow cannot feel original, and the author who cannot feel himself to be unique. If so, then the history of the novel is the history of originality both claimed and lost, of the local both exploded and occupied, of subjectivity both expanded and endangered, and finally the history of both the explosion of inwardness and the inner world's domination by exteriority. Above all today, when subjectivity also means the subject has hit a wall, that he sees his own threatened subjectivity, notices his own conquered locality, and can, in a sense, gaze into the face of his own deprivation.

To be sure, none of this explains the difference between Flaubert's objective austerity and Recaizade's grotesque humour, or why what was for the former a confession ('Madame Bovary, c'est moi') was for the latter an accusation levelled by others ('Ekrem is Bihruz, and there's an end to it'), or the difference between capitalism's near and distant provinces. I set out in this essay to assert not that literature on the periphery is governed by completely different laws but rather that characters living in different lands can meet in a similar universe of desire, that centre and periphery are always defined by one another. Girard's theory is less a theory of difference than of the surprising resemblances a similar psychological ground may produce in disparate localities. And it is, to a great extent, those surprising resemblances which carry the novel, despite all the local pressures it reflects, despite all the national-cultural anxieties at work in different locales, beyond the status of a national identity document. The novel is the modern ground shared by the Ottoman aristocrat and the provincial French bourgeois, the provincial French bourgeois and the nobleman of La Mancha, the nobleman of La Mancha and the Russian underground man, the Russian underground man and the disconnected Turk.

To return one last time to *The Carriage Affair*: though it sparkles with irony here and there, it is not an ironic novel. If it were, it would narrate a broken consciousness divided by irreconcilable voices. All the voices around Bihruz – not only Lamartine or Dumas but patriotic Namık Kemal, advocating a cheerful march toward progress; Muallim Naci, stubbornly defending the old literature; and the self-devouring will of Beşir Fuad, declaring war on Romanticism[24] – would have had to populate his consciousness; Bihruz Bey would have been racked by his lack of interiority. Tanpınar was right: like its hero, *The Carriage Affair* is a joke. The moment Bihruz Bey realizes that Periveş Hanım is a street tart, and what he thought love was a fiction, he gets into his carriage and speeds away from the scene. The novel ends there, just as it is really about to begin. But despite its weaknesses, *The Carriage Affair* marked a frontier from which there was no return for the Turkish novel. Even if with a grotesque joke Recaizade Ekrem succeeded in making his reader feel that for the Turkish writer *züppe*ry is not just an excess to be satirized but a foundational element of 'the *orijinal* Turkish spirit'; that the writer has always already tread that realm; and, perhaps most importantly of all, that the place known as the inner world is always already under threat. If we are to speak of a weakness in the modern Turkish novel, it is not a failure to return to the self but a failure to return enough; a failure to confront the countless uninvited guests there and face up to the reality that it is always already too late to return to the self.

I am thinking of an ironic scene in Oğuz Atay's *Dangerous Games*. The novel tells the story of the broken consciousness of 'emotional, romantic' Hikmet, author of the melodramas 'The

War of Rage against the Rules of Intellect' and 'Eastern Feeling Against Western Intellect'; in a sense, it is the story of Hikmet's division into several *hikmet*s.[25] In one of his endless dialogues with Hüsamettin Bey, Hikmet mentions a dream he had. In the dream he saw that crowd of Hikmets clearly for the first time and is thinking about writing an encyclopaedia to expound upon this. He will write first, and then they will take turns writing, each working without the knowledge of the others. At that point Hikmet makes the striking statement: 'They gave up on the idea because people in backward countries have no inner world.' Hüsamettin Bey asks, 'Who gave up on the idea?' Hikmet answers weakly: 'The British.'

'People in backward countries have no inner world.' The strength of Oğuz Atay's irony here comes, I think, of this statement's being both right and, of course, wrong. And Atay's singular place in Turkish literature comes of his having written about the condition of arriving onstage in the role of a servant, along with all the pain, rage and feelings of inadequacy that engenders; and of having written about all this inevitably pathetic psychic material while grappling both with an injured romanticism identified with the East, and directly with the problem of belatedness – not only the problem of a belatedly modernizing literature but the reality that all literature is always already belated in relation to experience. Only when the inner world can bear witness to its own emptiness, its own dependency, its own fundamental defectiveness, does it become an inner world. If there is such a thing as originality, it is reached by way of the ability to see the warping at the root; the inescapable defect which has already shaped the novel, the reader and the critic from the start. If Oğuz Atay is original, it is not in spite of this but precisely because of it.

I began this essay by saying that the ideal of originality had become a reflex in Turkish criticism. This is one of the reasons why it is so difficult to overcome. Once the desire for originality gives up on defining itself as problematic, it conceals the fact of the reaction against belatedness contained within it. That is why the various approaches I have mentioned all transact their business in a similar forgetting, albeit with differing political emphases. The first ('we have no novel of our own') uses the ideal of originality merely to hammer away at how homely we are; originality is always elsewhere. While the second ('let's return to ourselves') defines an original 'us', it in fact pretends not to see that this 'us' has long since been shaped by others, that the call to return to the self is a product of the pressure created by that external intervention anyway, and therefore the struggle to create a national literature, an original novel, an autonomous aesthetic culture, is always doomed to remain a belated strategy. In the first, the critic separates himself from his object entirely and takes on the role of guardian of an originality forever located abroad; in the second, the critic accuses writers of imitation while apparently never considering the reactive nature of his own claim to authenticity.

But criticism in Turkey, like the novel, was born in trauma. It tried to answer the question: 'Why do they have it and we don't?' It opened its eyes to love and hate nurtured for Europe, to admiration and to fear of the loss of self. In fact for that reason it is in the best position to understand the novel. Yet it keeps both the novel and itself back by jumping ahead to lean on the originality yardstick, continually handing the novel a bill of foreign debt as if criticism were made of other stuff. So, criticism would have much to gain if, rather than ruminate over 'the great lack', continually reproducing the languages of privation and victimhood, it pieced together its own national-cultural belatedness with the always already belatedness of the modern novel. For like the novel, criticism can move forward by bickering with its own unconditional admiration and rage, its self-regard as modern, original, authentic and its regard of others as primitive, imitation copies. The breakdown of criticism's *züppe* arrogance, and its provincial pride, must occur at a moment like this. It must be able to get out of this bind, and the way out leads through knowledge that it is long since bound.

As for the *Orijinal* Turkish Spirit. There is no need to say that there is much imitation in the *orijinal*, and goods to spare in the spirit. And the goods are, moreover, foreign goods.

Notes

INTRODUCTION

1. The phrase 'A Speaking Turkey' was coined by Süleyman Demirel, general chairman of the right-wing conservative-liberal Justice Party active in political life 1961–80. Demirel and other party leaders were prohibited from participating in political activity for seven years after the coup, and he expressed his demand for democracy by saying, 'We want a speaking Turkey, not a silent Turkey.' The media speedily transformed 'A Speaking Turkey' into a slogan symbolizing the desire for democracy. Demirel went on to become prime minister in 1991 and president of the Republic in 1993.
2. The State of Emergency Region Governorship was the martial law administration launched in 1983 to rule eight provinces of Turkey populated largely by Kurds. The governors were appointed by the Cabinet, attached to the Ministry of the Interior, and given state-of-emergency powers. The Governorship remained in force until 2002.
3. Georg Lukács, 'On the Nature and Form of the Essay', in *Soul and Form*, trans. Anna Bostock (Cambridge MA: MIT Press, 1971), pp. 1, 16–17.

ONE

1. Walter Benjamin, 'Surrealism: The Last Snapshot of the European Intelligentsia', in *Reflections*, trans. Edmund Jephcott (New York: Schocken, 1986), p. 180.
2. Quoted by Marshall Berman in *All That Is Solid Melts into Air: The Experience of Modernity* (London: Verso, 1983), pp. 165–7.

3. Georg Simmel, 'Metropolis and Mental Life', in *The Sociology of Georg Simmel*, ed. and trans. Kurt H. Wolff (New York: Free Press, 1950), p. 418.

4. Walter Benjamin, *Charles Baudelaire: A Lyric Poet in the Era of High Capitalism*, trans. Harry Zohn (London: New Left Books, 1973), p. 50.

5. Jerrold Seigel, *Bohemian Paris: Culture, Politics, and the Boundaries of Bourgeois Life, 1830–1930* (Baltimore MD: Johns Hopkins University Press, 1999), p. 107.

6. 'Arabesk' is a kind of pop music which had a large audience in Turkey from the late 1960s to the late 1990s. It embraces a variety of elements from classical, folk and light styles of Turkish music, and Arabic music as well, employing a variety of motifs from religion to political protest, and was banned from national television channels until the 1990s. Arabesk speaks of unrequited love, loss and despair, and, at least at first, addressed the losers in the big city. Orhan Gencebay is considered its creator, although he himself did not adopt the term, but in the 1980s and 1990s İbrahim Tatlıses was the most prolific of arabesk singers and enjoyed the greatest commercial success. For an in-depth analysis, see Meral Özbek, *Popüler Kültür ve Orhan Gencebay Arabeski* [Popular Culture and the Arabesk of Orhan Gencebay] (Istanbul: İletişim Yayıncılık, 1991). For a study in English, see Martin Stokes, *The Arabesk Debate: Music and Musicians in Modern Turkey* (Oxford: Clarendon Press, 1992).

7. Georg Simmel, 'The Stranger', in *The Sociology of Georg Simmel*, p. 402.

8. Murat Belge, 'Kültür Alışverişinde Uzun Yol Sürücüsü' [The Long-Distance Driver in Culture Traffic], *Cumhuriyet* [*The Republic* newspaper], 4 August 1982. The following is from Belge's *Tarihten Güncelliğe* [*From History to the Contemporary*] (Istanbul: Alan Yayıncılık, 1983), pp. 80–83: 'At first drivers left the radio on all the time, changing the channel when music came on that was alien to their culture. Drivers working routes after midnight in particular got into the habit of finding Arabic stations when the programming on Turkish stations ended for the night. I'd say that habit was an important bend in the road on the way to the invention of arabesk.'

9. Hilmi Yavuz, 'Lumpen Kültürü Üzerine: Ne o, Ne öteki!' [On Lumpen Culture: Neither One Nor the Other], in *Kültür Üzerine* [On Culture] (Istanbul: Bağlam Yayınları, 1987), pp. 99–103: 'The *lumpen* sees himself in a position determined by his lack of class and history: neither one nor the other. The Turkish *lumpen* sublates both rural culture and urban culture, the culture of both East and West. The correlation which determines the image of his life and identity is this: neither one nor the other.'

10. Umberto Eco, *A Theory of Semiotics* (Bloomington: Indiana University Press, 1976), p. 57.

11. Mustapha Khayati, 'Captive Words: Preface to a Situationist Dictionary', *Situationist International Anthology*, ed. and trans. Ken Knabb (Berkeley: Bureau of Public Secrets, 1981), p. 173.

12. Guy Debord, *Society of the Spectacle*, trans. Fredy Perlman and Jon Supak (Detroit: Black & Red, 1977), para. 34.

TWO

1. [The headscarf worn as a sign of veiling is called a 'turban'. It is usually accompanied by a raincoat to complete the modest public dress code. – *Trans.*]
2. Michel Foucault, *The History of Sexuality*, Volume 1: *An Introduction*, trans. Robert Hurley (New York: Vintage Books, 1980), p. 17.
3. Roland Barthes, 'Myth Today', in *Mythologies*, trans. Annette Lavers (London: Paladin, 1972), p. 150.
4. Ahmet Oktay, *Toplumsal Değişme ve Basın* [Social Transformation and the Press] (Istanbul: B/F/S Yayınları, 1987), pp. 108–9.
5. [Turkish also has an 'inferential' verb form (*–miş*), used when the speaker refers to an event he has not personally experienced. – *Trans.*]
6. Fredric Jameson, *Postmodernism, or, The Cultural Logic of Late Capitalism* (Durham NC: Duke University Press, 1991), p. 54.
7. Ibid., p. 25.
8. Nilüfer Göle, 'Yeni Sağ, Yeni Sol' [New Right, New Left], *Söz* [Speech], 3 December 1987.
9. ['Panama'da İç Kanama', literally 'Internal Bleeding in Panama', is the headline for an article about events in Panama and plays on the rhyme between 'Panama' and *kanama*, meaning 'haemorrhage; 'Katibime Cola'lı Gömlek', literally 'A Starched Shirt for my Secretary', is the headline for an article about Coca-Cola and plays on the rhyme between 'cola' and *kola*, meaning 'starch'; 'Türk Müziğinde Suna Kan Davası', literally 'The Suna Blood Feud in Turkish Music', is an interview with the violinist Suna Kan and, although the interview has nothing to do with a blood feud, plays on the fact that the violinist's last name, 'Kan', means 'blood', and that the word *dava*, meaning 'claim' or 'court case', takes on the meaning 'feud' when used in the phrase *kan davası*; 'Dalyan'ın Kerataları', literally 'Dalyan's Rascals', is the headline for an article on the endangered species of *Carreta carreta* sea turtles living off the coast of Dalyan and plays on the rhyme between the name of the turtle and the word *kerata*, meaning 'rascal'. – *Trans.*]

THREE

1. Jean Bethke Elshtain, *The Public Man, The Private Woman* (Princeton NJ: Princeton University Press, 1981); Hannah Arendt, *The Human Condition* (Chicago: University of Chicago Press, 1958).
2. Paul Veyne, 'The Roman Empire', in *A History of Private Life: From Pagan Rome to Byzantium*, ed. Paul Veyne et al. (Cambridge MA: Belknap Press, Harvard University Press 1992), vol. 1, p. 163.

3. Ferit Devellioğlu, *Osmanlıca-Türkçe Ansiklopedik Lûgat* [Ottoman-Turkish Encyclopedic Dictionary] (Ankara: Aydın Kitabevi, rev. edn, 1993).

4. Lewis Mumford wrote of how in the seventeenth century servants still slept in the same room as their masters. All the rooms in the house were interconnected and alike; they had not yet acquired distinct boundaries or special functions. People ate, slept, worked, received guests and relaxed all in the same room. Private life and the life shared with strangers had not yet been transformed into separate, inviolable spheres, delineated by separate rooms. But a hundred years later, space within the home had become differentiated. In homes with many rooms, built on smaller pieces of real estate, rooms began to be 'lined up along corridors as houses were lined up along streets'; they gave onto a corridor, not onto each other. The privacy of the bourgeois family required that visitors give advance notice of their coming and servants be summoned with bells. Servants were banished from table and children from their parents' bedroom. The acquisition by the family of private, spiritual meaning beyond the moral and social was a product of the same period. Lewis Mumford, *The City in History: Its Origins, Its Transformations, and Its Prospects* (Harmondsworth: Penguin, 1961), p. 439.

5. Richard Sennett, *The Fall of Public Man* (New York: W.W. Norton, 1992).

6. Jürgen Habermas writes of a similar transformation in *The Structural Transformation of the Public Sphere* (Cambridge MA: MIT Press, 1991). He says that the public sphere declined in terms of its function, although as a domain it had been expanding for almost a century. For Habermas 'the public sphere' means a bourgeois public sphere distinguished from the representative publicity of the palace and based on commodity exchange, social labour and social reproduction. But this new domain was also a rational-critical sphere which reasoning individuals, invested with their experience of the private realm, formed against public power. This was the potential Habermas believes no longer exists in our day: the public sphere declined with the centralization of capital, the socialization of the state, and the state-ification of society. The laws of the market invaded the sphere set aside for individuals; the public of rational consensus became a passive consumer community; the relationship once established between privacy and literacy dissolved; and the public domain was transformed into a sphere where private life stories were announced to all, a spectral, manipulative publicity.

7. Yakup Kadri Karaosmanoğlu (1889–1974), known for his political as well as literary career, was an important author of the Turkish Republican period. His most famous novels are *Kiralık Konak* [Mansion for Rent], 1922; *Hüküm Gecesi* [The Night of the Verdict], 1927; *Sodom ve Gomore* [Sodom and Gomorrah], 1928; *Yaban* [Stranger], 1932; and *Ankara*, 1934.

8. 'The Gate of Felicity' was one of the names by which the Ottoman capital was known.

9. This is a line from a song sung in schools on 23 April, anniversary of the first convening of the Turkish parliament, celebrated in Turkey as a children's festival. The word *kamutay*, from *kamu*, 'public', signifies the parliament.

10. For a detailed study of how the ideology of objectivity in news reporting was delegitimized and the announcer's sincerity became the guarantee of truth in news, see Margaret Morse, 'The Television News Personality and Credibility', in *Studies in Entertainment: Critical Approaches to Mass Culture*, ed. Tania Modleski (Bloomington: Indiana University Press, 1986), pp. 55–80.

11. The Turkish National Radio-Television (Türk Radyo Televizyon) Institution was the sole institution broadcasting radio and television programming until the founding of private radio and television stations in the early 1990s.

12. İlber Ortaylı, *İstanbul'dan Sayfalar* [Pages from Istanbul] (İstanbul: Hil Yayın, 1986), pp. 212–13.

FOUR

1. Fredric Jameson, 'Periodizing the 60s', in *The Ideologies of Theory: Essays 1971–1986*, Volume 2: *Syntax of History* (London: Routledge, 1988), pp. 180–81.

2. [After Mustafa Kemal Atatürk. – *Trans.*]

3. Jean-François Lyotard, *The Postmodern Condition: A Report on Knowledge* (Minneapolis: University of Minnesota Press, 1984), p. 87.

FIVE

1. What should be emphasized here is that Orhan Gencebay's dichotomy of abandon and discipline, outcry and decorum, was united in a 'big brother' image that his audience found authentic. Its antithesis was the homosexual 'sun of art' image Zeki Müren presented in Turkey during the 1960s. There was a dichotomy in that image as well, but the two faces making it up always remained two separate parts. Zeki Müren spoke an exaggerated version of old Istanbul gentlemanly diction, excessively refined and dainty, while concealing a penchant for obscene profanity beneath it all. In his films he played the role of the handsome young leading man, but in dream scenes he suddenly appeared before viewers clad in wispy veils, chiffons and sequinned lamé. Zeki Müren went back and forth between exaggerated delicacy and slang, false modesty and degeneracy, gentlemanliness and effeminacy. This is partly what made him both Turkey's 'sun of art' and its clown. Later we saw a caricature version of the same cleavage in the transsexual singer Bülent Ersoy. He also could not talk without throwing in Ottoman-esque phrases of false politesse, but when he lost his temper there would flow out of him atrocious profanities in bestial slang. The authenticity Turkish society begrudges those of its stars who are

not 'big brothers': two separate worlds always to be made of irreconcilably separate identities.

2. This difference is felt even in Gencebay's songs of the 1980s. Meral Özbek writes of how Gencebay's songs of the 1980s lost some of the tension those of his 1970s 'transcendental' period had; he began to take up desire in its more worldly, concrete, specific aspects and employed more joyful, jumpier rhythms. The desire invested in unrequited love began to unravel and seek out more realistic targets. There was a transition from 'Lovers are never happy' to 'I'll forget you and find someone else to love'. *Popüler Kültür ve Orhan Gencebay Arabeski* [Popular Culture and the Arabesk of Orhan Gencebay], (Istanbul: İletişim Yayıncılık, 1991), pp. 208–11.

3. 'Me Too' might bring to mind the French slogan of 1968, 'We want it all and we want it now!' There is doubtless an important difference of context here; the '68 slogan was first of all a political slogan. But it should not be forgotten that the moment it lost its connection to its political content, it became the slogan of a consumer society calling people to take pleasure in this world right now. We should also not forget that, shouted in Europe almost twenty years prior to the period discussed here, the slogan found its audience in Turkey only in the 1980s, and, after a short political life, was embellished with local colour to arrive at a destination not all that far from 'Me Too'. That is why I say Gencebay's 'Let this World Sink', his investment not in 'right now' but in a distant future, represents a certain restraint if not an anachronistic resistance against consumer society.

4. If precise figures are required, of the 195 films made in 1979, 131 were sex films. Giovanni Scognamillo, *Türk Sinema Tarihi* [History of Turkish Cinema], Volume 2: *1960–1986* (Istanbul: Metis Yayınları, 1988).

5. [The Turkish title, 'Şehvet (lust) Kurbanı Şevket', relies on a characteristically neat onomatopoeia. – *Trans.*]

6. Slavoj Žižek may provide clues to the difference between a 'normal' romantic film or melodrama and a pornographic movie: '[I]n a "normal," nonpornographic film, a love scene is always built around a certain insurmountable limit; "all cannot be shown." At a certain point the image is blurred, the camera moves off, the scene is interrupted, we never directly see "that" (the penetration of the organs etc.). In contrast to this limit of representability defining the "normal" love story or melodrama, pornography goes beyond, it "shows everything." The paradox is, however, that by trespassing the limit, it always *goes too far*, i.e., it *misses* what remains concealed in a "normal," nonpornographic love scene.' In other words, in a film about love there is a story and desire remains unsatisfied; in a pornographic film narrative is an excuse to 'get down to business', so there is not really a story. In the first, desire is always to come, while in the second it is always long since past. Perhaps we could also say that desire in not in fact located in either but precisely in

the tension created by the combination of both worlds and the fact that they never really coincide. *Looking Awry: An Introduction to Jacques Lacan through Popular Culture* (Cambridge MA: MIT Press, 1991), p. 110.

7. 'Second generation' pornographic magazines like *Playboy* and *Penthouse* began their publication life in Turkey in the second half of the 1980s. It is truly interesting that, with their very first issues, they embarked on a mission of arguing against the left discourse which had long since lost its cultural power, and positioned themselves as offering a promise of freedom contradicting it. I am truly curious as to whether pornographic magazines in other countries have ever taken on such a mission.

8. For an article comparing the asocial, abnormal 'voyeur' culture of the 1970s, nourished on secrecy and shame, with the 'social exhibitionism' which began to become a modern norm in the 1980s, see Yaşar Çabuklu, 'Röntgencilik' [Exhibitionism], in his *Kovulanın İzi* [The Trail of the Rejected] (Istanbul: Metis Yayınları, 2001), pp. 104–11.

9. Sigmund Freud, *Civilization and its Discontents*, trans. and ed. James Stratchey (New York: W.W. Norton, 1961), p. 37.

SIX

1. Philippe Ariès, *Western Attitudes toward Death: From Middle Ages to the Present* (Baltimore MD: Johns Hopkins University Press, 1974).

2. 'Return to Life' was the official name of the operation carried out by approximately 10,000 security forces in twenty prisons simultaneously on 19 December 2000 after inmates who had launched a hunger strike in protest against the institution of the F-Type cell system began to starve themselves to death. Thirty detainees and prisoners lost their lives during the operation, shot or burned to death or overcome by smoke inhalation. Hundreds more were wounded. The resistance was suppressed and the F-Type cell system instituted following the operation.

3. The 'Return to Life Operation' was also officially called 'The Compassion Operation'.

4. Geoffrey Gorer, *Death, Grief and Mourning* (London: Cresset Press, 1965). 'The Pornography of Death' is included in the book.

5. Georges Bataille, 'Michelet', in *Literature and Evil*, trans. Alastair Hamilton (New York: Marion Boyars, 1997).

SEVEN

1. Murat Belge, 'Bir Poster' [A Poster], in *Tarihten Güncelliğe* [From History to Contemporaneity] (Istanbul: Alan Yayıncılık, 1983), pp. 265–9.

2. 'Yeşilçam' is the name of a street in the Beyoğlu neighbourhood of Istanbul

where most film companies had their offices prior to 1980. Turkish cinema of that era came to be known after the street.

3. Kemalettin Tuğcu (1902–1996) wrote more than 500 novels for children, starting in the 1950s, and was the leading author of popular children's literature in Turkey.

4. Oğuz Atay (1934–1977), known for his novels *Tutunamayanlar* (The Disconnected) and *Tehlikeli Oyunlar* (Dangerous Games), is one of the greatest authors of modernist Turkish literature. Atay gained a much wider audience in the 1980s when themes of marginality began to become popular in Turkey and readers embraced him as the creator of a 'cult of the disconnected'. Ece Eyhan (1931–2002) was one of the modern masters of Turkish poetry.

5. 'Woman of Agony' was a very popular song by the singer Bergen, famed in the 1980s as the 'Queen of Arabesk'. The phrase was later identified with Bergen herself, who really did have an agonized life. Her jealous husband threw acid in her face one night while she was onstage, blinding her in one eye, and later shot her dead at the age of 28 in 1989.

6. Nezih Erdoğan emphasized in his article 'Ulusal Kimlik, Kolonyal Söylem ve Yeşilçam Melodramı' [National Identity, Colonial Discourse and Yeşilçam Melodrama] (*Toplum ve Bilim* 67, Summer 1995) that in Yeşilçam films it was usually female village immigrants to the city who represented 'low-class' values like simplicity, honesty and loyalty to those who mistreated them. I believe the change that had occurred by the 1990s and the reasons why this oppressed but honest, despised but proud, character was then more often male are worth investigating.

7. Doğuş grew up on the streets and became famous for his sad songs in the 1990s. He spent time in prison for rape.

8. For a sociological and psychoanalytic analysis of the idea of the oppressed subject in Turkish political life, particularly in Turk–Islam synthesis theory, see Fethi Açıkel, '"Kutsal Mazlumluğun" Psikopatolojisi' [The Psychopathology of "Sacred Oppression"], *Toplum ve Bilim* 40, Summer 1996. Açıkel claimed that this discourse of suffering and torment he characterized as the Turkish Republic's 'second modernization discourse' represented a claim to power, and a propensity for rage and revenge, on the part of the masses who had lost their class, cultural and symbolic supports to the violence of late capitalism. So while the discourse of oppression gave voice to underdevelopment, it also set in motion a discourse of rigour, greatness and power ('great Turkey', 'glorious history', 'showing the world the power of the Turk'). That was also why it was articulated to an oppressive political apparatus.

9. Ariès made clear that what he called 'the discovery of childhood' occurred among the middle classes. The poor were always rather marginal to this event, for several reasons. Because the death rate for children in poor families was high, they were not regarded as a continuous presence and so could not become

a separate centre of attraction as they did in middle-class families. Further-more, since children of poor families had to work, they entered the world of adults much sooner; they became acquainted with the factory, the workplace, the army barracks, the police station, the street and the reform school at an early age. All of this prevented childhood from being separated clearly from the world of adults. Philippe Ariès, *Centuries of Childhood* (London: Peregrine Books, 1986), pp. 30–130.

10. According to Andreas Huyssen, fear of the masses is so strong because it is fed by much more ancient fears, in particular fear of women. The bourgeois fear of the mob has in many cases been intertwined with man's fear of woman. Throughout the nineteenth and twentieth centuries, when the masses consti-tuted a political threat in Western Europe, they were defined as a hysterical, raging mob, an engulfing flood of rebellion, with images of the red whore at the barricades. The first theoreticians of mass culture in this period persistently defined mass culture as an effeminate, devouring and irrational thing, as a seductive, evil queen whose attraction must be resisted. In that fear of the mob there is dread not only of the political and social threat formed by the masses but of unrestrained nature, sexuality, the unconscious, and loss of stable ego boundaries as well. Andreas Huyssen, 'Mass Culture as Woman: Modernism's Other', in *After the Great Divide: Modernism, Mass Culture, Postmodernism* (Bloomington: Indiana University Press, 1987), pp. 44–65.

EIGHT

1. Ahmet Hamdi Tanpınar (1901–1962), *Huzur* (Istanbul: Dergâh Yayınları, 1949); English translation by Erdağ Göknar, *A Mind at Peace* (New York: Archipelago Books, 2008).

2. Fethi Naci and Mehmet Kaplan are in accord in viewing Suad as a character out of Dostoevsky. See Fethi Naci, *Yüzyılın Yüz Romanı* [A Hundred Novels of the Century] (Istanbul: Adam Yayınları, 1999, p. 249; and Mehmet Kaplan, 'Bir Şairin Romanı: Huzur' [A Poet's Novel] *Türk Dili ve Edebiyatı Dergisi* [Journal of Turkish Language and Literature] 31, December 1962, pp. 37–8. It was Fethi Naci who drew attention to the similarity between the suicides of Suad and Stavrogin, and who called Suad's a 'translated suicide'. Later Berna Moran would join in on the 'translated suicide' idea, calling attention to the similarity between Suad's suicide and that of the character Spandrell in Aldous Huxley's *Point Counter Point*: Spandrell hanged himself to the accompaniment of Beethoven's Quartet in A minor. But Moran also said the similarity was no accident, pointing out that the character Mümtaz loved Huxley. See Berna Moran, 'Bir Huzursuzluğun Romanı' [Novel of an Unpeaceful Mind], *Türk Romanına Eleştirel Bir Bakış* [A Critical View of the Turkish Novel] (Istanbul: İletişim Yayınları , 2nd edn, 1987), vol. 1, pp. 274–5.

3. Tanpınar was influenced by Dostoevsky, but had grown tired of him by the time he wrote *A Mind at Peace*. Although he mentioned the greatness of Dostoevsky in an article, 'The Novelist Confronted by Life', he also said: 'I am sick of commonplace Russian novels and short stories. Just as I am sick of wound-up watches and every maddening ticking thing driven by a coil spring they have behind them instead of a human being... Those underground confessions, those possessed men, those great suffering egos whose subjectivity yawns open like a well of perdition, their lack of will, that intoxication with misery and suffering, that irreparable wretchedness – I can no longer get comfortably intoxicated by such things. Those madmen seem to me to lack elegance, I immediately find the mechanized side of their despair', *Edebiyat Üzerine Makaleler* [Writings on Literature] (Istanbul: Dergâh Yayınları, 3rd edn, 1992), p. 54.

4. Orhan Koçak, in 'Kaptırılmış İdeal: *Mai ve Siyah* Üzerine Psikanalitik Bir Deneme' ['Missed Ideal: A Psychoanalytic Essay on *The Blue and the Black*'], pointed out that Tanpınar too was one of the critics who accused New Literature [Edebiyat-ı Cedide] authors, Halit Ziya in particular, of aestheticism, a lack of roots and 'distance' – of allowing himself to be fascinated by influences from abroad, by foreign, borrowed ideals. Tanpınar criticized Halit Ziya for a kind of Bovaryism, for giving voice to acquired or imitated desires rather than being sincere, natural and spontaneous: *Toplum ve Bilim* [Society and Science] 70, Summer 1996, pp. 94–150.

5. According to Fethi Naci, this sentence demonstrates that Tanpınar was aware of this 'linguistic' weakness of his. *Yüzyılın Yüz Romanı*, p. 252. According to Berna Moran, Tanpınar used this exaggerated style in order better to narrate Mümtaz's attitude, experience and aestheticism, and thereby expose it to criticism. Moran, *Türk Romanına Eleştirel Bir Bakış*, p. 273.

6. Şerif Mardin, "Aydınlar' Konusunda Ülgener ve Bir İzah Denemesi' [Ülgener on the Subject of Intellectuals, and an Experiment in Commentary], *Toplum ve Bilim* 24, 1984, pp. 9–16; 'Super-Westernization in Urban Life in the Ottoman Empire in the Last Quarter of the Nineteenth Century', in Peter Benedict, Erol Tümertekin and Fatma Mansur (eds), *Turkey: Geographic and Social Perspectives* (Leiden: Brill, 1974), pp. 403–46.

   The thesis that Turkish Literature has never had its share of creative evil, is incapable of tragedy, has a superficial sense of the fantastic, and is therefore stunted in its growth has been echoed in many other writings, and more often than not used as a universal key to open every door.

7. Such is the case in, for example, Giovanni Scognamillo and Arif Arslan's *Doğu ve Batı Kaynaklarına Göre Şeytan* [Satan according to Eastern and Western Sources] (Istanbul: Karizma Yayınları, 1999).

8. Bernstein's concept of the abject, which he developed in relation to the depraved nephew type in Diderot's dialogue *Rameau's Nephew* and characters of

Dostoevsky's differs from Julia Kristeva's psychoanalytic concept in *Powers of Horror*, where she makes use of Mary Douglas's anthropological studies on primitive societies and others on India, and exemplifies it with reference to the works of Louis-Ferdinand Céline. Kristeva's abject is a more general concept with psychological, cultural, literary and religious resonances. Bernstein expains how a specific literary type which emerged in a specific historical period became a type of depravity, misery and scandal. Michael André Bernstein, *Bitter Carnival: Ressentiment and the Abject Hero* (Princeton NJ: Princeton University Press, 1992); Julia Kristeva, *Powers of Horror: An Essay on Abjection* (New York: Columbia University Press, 1982).

9. Bernstein, *Bitter Carnival*, p. 118.

10. We are confronted again by this 'precious shit' when we return two centuries later to Rameau's city of Paris. Now it is Jean Genet who defines poetry as 'the art of using shit and making you eat it'. 'Poetry consisted in transforming subjects taken to be vile into subjects accepted as noble, and this with the help of language.' Genet tries to take his revenge by creating Sublime Evil out of Sublime Good France; he tries to infect the minds of good citizens with the savage object he creates, transforming his damnedness into a posture and himself into an object of hatred. But here what makes him 'abject' in the sense we have discussed – more perhaps than the fact that he was lionized for his defence of being a damned shit, that he claimed he took pleasure in the ruin of victors, and continued his profession of thievery in earning considerable royalties from his books – is that he saw no harm in agreeing that he said all of this with prideful resentment ('I don't give a damn'), did not hesitate to characterize the decision to be evil as naive, romantic, even stupid; and, more importantly, that he felt the championing of evil was something that could always be 'recuperated' – 'It means living Evil in such a way that you are not recuperated by the social forces that symbolize the Good.' To all of this should be added his sense that an artist can never be entirely destructive: 'The very concern with creating a harmonious sentence supposes a morality, that is, a relation between the author and a possible reader. I write in order to be read. No one writes for nothing.' Jean Genet, 'Interview with Madeline Gobeil', in *The Declared Enemy: Texts and Interviews*, ed. Albert Dichy, trans. Jeff Fort (Palo Alto CA: Stanford University Press, 2004), pp. 2–18.

11. Perhaps the worst accusation that can be levelled at the lawless bad boy, and he can level at himself, is banality. For to be banal is to be like everyone else, to be merely a cliché, to obey the law. 'The Banality of Evil' was the subtitle of Hannah Arendt's book about the Nazi officer Adolf Eichmann, who played an active role in the killing of millions of Jews. Eichmann was tried in Jerusalem in 1960 and after the two year-long trial was condemned to death and hanged. By 'banality' Arendt meant that while during his trial everyone wanted to think of Eichmann as a diabolical monster, he was nothing like

the evil characters we encounter in literature. He was not Iago, Macbeth or Richard III. He had no characteristically evil pride, no mocking contempt for the law, nor any diabolical depth with which to challenge those judging him. (He was not, for example, like Charles Manson, who was mythologized as a media hero for his anti-social statements ten years later during his trial in Los Angeles, and in that respect 'succeeded' in becoming an American Raskolnikov devoid of internal conflict, guilt or spiritual suffering.) On the contrary, he was exceedingly normal, even typical; he was an ordinary civil servant. This man, responsible for the most extraordinary crimes in the world, had committed them out of the most ordinary motives – because he wanted to be a good citizen, in an effort to rise in his profession, out of a sense of duty and his belief in a decent society. In Eichmann there was no transgressiveness, no lawlessness or irregularity; on the contrary, he had been obedient to the law from the start. And this is what so shocked everyone; Eichmann's speech betrayed no diabolical cleverness, merely an incredible banality. Even his final words before judgment was passed were filled with the proud clichés of cheerful obedience to the law. This, according to Arendt, was the lesson of the Jerusalem trial. Eichmann had shown the entire world the inconceivably gruesome, unspeakable banality of evil, and this banality, practised in a society organized on criminal principles, had brought greater calamity to the world than the sum of all evil impulses which naturally exist in man. Hannah Arendt, *Eichmann in Jerusalem: A Report on the Banality of Evil* (Harmondsworth: Penguin, 1963).

12. Orhan Pamuk draws attention to something similar in an essay on Dostoevsky, 'Aşağılanmanın Zevkleri' [The Pleasures of being Belittled], *Radikal İki*, 9 July 2000. According to Pamuk, what gives *Notes from Underground* its real energy is 'envy, rage and pride at not being European'.There is a dilemma here: like his character, Dostoevsky studied in Europe and was aware that he owed his existence to Westernization, above all that he was emplying a Western art form. But, on the other hand, he feels anger towards those who find success, legitimacy or happiness in Westernism. According to Pamuk, *Notes from Underground* is in this respect the product of the 'destructive tension' Dostoevsky felt in 'his affinity for European thought and his rage against it, in being European and defying Europe'.

There is doubtless an aspect to Dostoevsky which goes beyond this and many other interpretations. But in my opinion Orhan Pamuk's observations are correct in that they emphasize something generally overlooked in other Dostoevsky criticism. But there is a second truth within the first: Pamuk's interpretation of Dostoevsky is itself a product of the dilemma which constitutes the topic of interpretation. Orhan Pamuk is one of Turkey's most Western authors; he was Western-educated, he owes his existence to Westernization, and he employs a Western art form; yet despite this, he cannot escape being a Turk in the West and having to comment upon Turkish politics as he is subjected to journalists' questions about Turkey. In my opinion 'The Pleasures of being Belittled' is an important piece because it gives voice to Pamuk's own 'destructive tension' as much as it tries to explain Dostoevsky's.

13. Orhan Koçak, 'Kaptırılmış İdeal: *Mai ve Siyah* Üzerine Psikanalitik Bir Deneme', p. 147. For another essay of Koçak's dealing with similar theses, see '"Our Master, the Novice": On the Catastrophic Births of Modern Turkish Poetry', *Relocating the Fault Lines: Turkey Beyond the East–West Divide*, South Atlantic Quarterly, vol. 102, no. 2/3, Spring/Summer 2003, pp. 567–98.

14. Gregory Jusdanis, *Belated Modernity and Aesthetic Culture: Inventing National Literature* (Minneapolis: University of Minnesota Press, 1991), pp. 78–84, 163.

15. That the common mode of literary and cultural criticism in Turkey is based on a proof of absence is a result of the same bind. The list of things lacking is long: 'There is no tragedy in Turkey', 'There is no novel in Turkey', 'There is no intellectual life in Turkey', 'There is no criticism in Turkey.' Is it not a product of the same obession that while Western critics struggle persistently with an excess of meaning and presence, intellectuals in Turkey persistently complain of a lack and, furthermore, derive their authority as critics from the proof of absence?

16. Bernstein, *Bitter Carnival*, p. 112.

17. [*Sahtegi* denotes false action, its result or its instrument; *muannit* means 'obstinate, unyielding'. So, the name of the character Bay Muannit Sahtegi could be translated literally as 'Mr Unyielding Inauthenticity'. – *Trans.*]

18. Citizens blow their car horns during the ceremonies marking the anniversery of Mustafa Kemal Atatürk's death on 10 November.

NINE

1. Martin Jay, 'The Uncanny Nineties', in *Cultural Semantics: Keywords of Our Time* (Amherst: University of Massachusetts Press, 1998), pp. 157–65.

TEN

1. Gregory Jusdanis, *Belated Modernity and Aesthetic Culture: Inventing National Literature* (Minneapolis: University of Minnesota Press, 1991).

2. Daryush Shayegan, *Le regard mutilé: schizophrénie culturelle: pays traditionnels face à la modernité* (Paris: Albin Michel, 1989), p. 83.

3. Jale Parla has argued that the Turkish novel was born into fatherlessness not only because the first Turkish novels were about fatherless boys, but also because the first novelists were men who had had to assume the role of the father at an early age, and become 'authorative children' in order to compensate

Notes

for the lack of political-intellectual power in the society at large. Jale Parla, *Babalar ve Oğullar* [Fathers and Sons] (Istanbul: İletişim Yayınları, 1990).

4. Orhan Koçak, 'Kaptırılmış İdeal: *Mai ve Siyah* Üzerine Psikanalitik Bir Deneme' [Missed Ideal: A Psychoanalytic Essay on *The Blue and the Black*], *Toplum ve Bilim* [Society and Knowledge] 70, Summer 1996, pp. 94–152. I will discuss Koçak's views later in this essay.

5. For Tanpınar's views on this subject, see *Edebiyat Üzerine Makaleler* [Articles on Literature] (Istanbul: Dergâh Yayınları, 3rd edn, 1992); 'Bizde Roman [Our Novel]: 1 and 2', pp. 45–52; 'Milli Bir Edebiyata Doğru' [Towards a National Literature], pp. 86–9; 'Türk Edebiyatında Cereyanlar' [Movements in Turkish Literature], pp. 119–20; and 'Ahmet Hamdi Tanpınar'la Bir Konuşma' [A Conversation with Ahmet Hamdi Tanpınar], in *Yaşadığım Gibi* [As I have Lived] (Istanbul: Dergâh Yayınları, 1996).

6. 'Milli Bir Edebiyata Doğru', p. 91.

7. Oğuz Atay was an important author of the Turkish modernist novel and a master of irony. His two most important works are *Tutunamayanlar* [The Disconnected] and *Tehlikeli Oyunlar* [Dangerous Games].

8. [Köprülü's spelling, *orijinal*, was a Turkish phoneticization of the French *original*. – Trans.]

9. *Atatürk Devri Fikir Hayatı* [The Intellectual Life of the Ataturk Period], ed. Mehmet Kaplan et al. (Ankara: Kültür Bakanlığı Yayınları, 1981), vol. 2, pp. 131–3.

10. Ian Watt, *The Rise of the Novel* (Harmondsworth: Penguin, new edn, 1972), p. 15.

11. Cemil Meriç, *Kırk Ambar* [Forty Storehouses], Volume 1: *Rümuz-ül Edeb* [The Signs of Literature] (Istanbul: Ötüken Neşriyat, 1980; new edn Iletişim Yayınları, 1998), p. 322.

12. The Turkish term *züppe* has the meanings of both 'dandy' and 'snob'. The *züppe* snob blatantly imitates the 'superior' other he longs to be near while rebuffing those regarded as inferior. But dandyism is marked also by an exaggerated attention to personal appearance, an affectation of cold indifference and pretension to self-sufficiency calculated to rouse in others the desire the dandy pretends to feel for himself. As René Girard puts it, the dandy practices an '*askesis* for the sake of desire', thereby acting as a 'magnet' for the unattached desires of others. In *The Carriage Affair*, Bihruz is both a snob and a Westernized dandy: obsessed with mirrors, he is scrupulously attentive to his appearance, and while he obviously imitates the 'superior' other, he dismisses his own culture as inferior. For a discussion of literary dandyism within the broader context of snobbery, see René Girard, *Deceit, Desire, and the Novel: Self and Other in Literary Structure*, trans. Yvonne Freccero (Baltimore MD: Johns Hopkins University Press, 1988), pp. 162–4. For the transformations of the *züppe* figure in Turkish literature, see Berna

Moran, 'Alafranga Züppeden Alafranga Haine' [From alla franga Züppe to alla franga Villain], *Türk Romanına Eleştirel Bir Bakış* [A Critical Look at the Turkish Novel] (Istanbul: İletişim Yayınları, 2nd edn, 1987), pp. 250–59. On how the *züppe* figure in Ottoman Turkish literature expressed effeminization anxiety, see Nurdan Gürbilek, 'Kadınsılaşma Endişesi: Efemine Erkekler, Hadım Oğullar, Kadın-Adamlar' [Effeminization Anxiety: Effeminate Men, Castrated Sons, Womanish Men], in *Kör Ayna, Kayıp Şark: Edebiyat ve Endişe* [Blind Mirror, Lost East: Literature and Anxiety] (Istanbul: Metis Yayınları, 2004), pp. 53–74.

13. Ahmet Hamdi Tanpınar, 'Romana ve Romancıya Dair Notlar III' [Notes on the Novel and the Novelist III] and 'Recâi Zâde Mahmud Ekrem', in *Edebiyat Üzerine Makaleler* [Articles on Literaure], pp. 67, 248–53; 'Recâi Zâde Mahmut Ekrem Bey', in *19. Asır Türk Edebiyatı Tarihi* [History of Nineteenth-Century Turkish Literature](Istanbul: İstanbul Üniversitesi Edebiyat Fakültesi Yayınları, 2nd edn, 1956), vol. 1, pp. 467–96.

14. Şerif Mardin, 'Tanzimat'tan Sonra Aşırı Batılılaşma', in *Türk Modernleşmesi* [Turkish Modernization] (Istanbul: İletişim Yayınları, 8th edn, 2000), pp. 21–79; 'Super-Westernization in Urban Life in the Ottoman Empire in the Last Quarter of the Nineteenth Century', in Peter Benedict, Erol Tümertekin and Fatma Mansur (eds), *Turkey: Geographic and Social Perspectives* (Leiden: Brill, 1974), pp. 403–46.

15. Jale Parla, 'Metinler Labirentinde Bir Sevda: Araba Sevdası' [Passion in the Labyrinth of Texts: *The Carriage Affair*], in *Babalar ve Oğullar* [Fathers and Sons], pp. 105–24; 'İstanbul'da İki Don Kişot: Meczup Okurdan Saf Okura' [Two Don Quixotes in Istanbul: Readers Lunatic and Naive], in *Berna Moran'a Armağan: Türk Edebiyatına Eleştirel Bir Bakış* [Presented to Berna Moran: A Critical Look at Turkish Literature] (Istanbul: İletişim Yayınları, 1997), pp. 206–9; and 'Car Narratives: A Subgenre in Turkish Novel Writing', *Relocating the Fault Lines: Turkey beyond the East–West Divide*, South Atlantic Quarterly, vol. 102, no. 2/3, Spring/Summer 2003, pp. 535–50.

16. *Edebiyâta Dair* [Regarding Literature] (Istanbul: Yahya Kemal Enstitüsü Yayınları, 2nd edn, 1984), pp. 288–90.

17. Henri Lefebvre, *La vie quotidienne dans le monde moderne* (Paris: Gallimard, 1968), pp. 191–6.

18. Parla has written that *The Carriage Affair* is 'a textual negation of the idea' that two opposing epistemological systems allowing no possibility of reconciliation 'can coexist at the same time'. *Babalar ve Oğullar*, p. 103.

19. Jules de Gautier, 'Le Bovarysme' (Paris: Éditions du Sandre, 2007).

20. René Girard, *Deceit, Desire and the Novel: Self and Other in Literary Structure*, trans. Yvonne Freccero (Baltimore and London: Johns Hopkins University Press, 1966).

21. Franco Moretti, *The Way of the World: The Bildungsroman in European Culture*,

trans. Albert Sbragia (London: Verso, 2000), pp. 164–9. In the chapter 'Dialectics of Desire', Moretti writes of how 'the desiring subject', which was regarded in the 1970s as a delegitimizing, even subversive, force, was a product of the capitalist metropole.

22. Ibid., p. 173.

23. The similarities between *The Carriage Affair* and *Madame Bovary* are not the result of influence. Flaubert's ideas were not among those racing through Istanbul like an infectious disease when Ekrem was growing up; Flaubert's name shows up in Tanzimat debates at a later date. The 'shaykh of the profession of realism' was introduced to Turkish readers by Ali Kemal, author of *Edebiyyat-ı Hakikiyye Dersleri* [Lessons in the Literature of Realism] and Ahmet Şuayb, author of *Hayat ve Kitaplar* [Life and Books], a collection of his essays and reviews published earlier in the renowned *Servet-i Fünun* magazine. See Cemil Meriç, *Kırk Ambar*, p. 298, and Beşir Ayvazoğlu, *Geleneğin Direnişi* [The Resistance of Tradition] (Istanbul: Ötüken Yayınları, 1997), pp. 115–16.

24. Beşir Fuad (1852–1887), known as 'the first Turkish materialist' and 'the first Turkish positivist', was an atheist thinker and author who wrote criticism defending naturalism against writers influenced by Romanticism. He commited suicide by slitting his wrists, recording what he experienced as a scientific experiment until he expired.

25. Hikmet, the character's name, has the meanings of 'knowledge', 'inner knowledge' and 'wisdom'.

Index

Index

Index